# WALK ON!

# DONALD M. JOY

A DIVISION OF SCRIPTURE PRESS PUBLICATIONS INC.
USA CANADA ENGLAND

## Spiritual Formation Series

| | |
|---|---|
| *Embrace the Spirit* | Steven Harper |
| *Cry Joy!* | Jerry Mercer |
| *Walk On!* | Donald Joy |
| *Celebrate, My Soul!* | Reginald Johnson |

Scripture quotations, unless otherwise noted, are from the *Holy Bible, New International Version*, © 1973, 1978, 1984, International Bible Society. Used by permission of Zondervan Bible Publishers. Other quotations are from the *King James Version* (KJV); the *Revised Standard Version of the Bible* (RSV), © 1946, 1952, 1971, 1973; *The Living Bible* (TLB), © 1971, Tyndale House Publishers, Wheaton, IL 60189. Used by permission.

Recommended Dewey Decimal Classification: 248.3.
Suggested Subject Heading: SPIRITUAL LIFE

Library of Congress Catalog Card Number: 88-60225
ISBN: 0-89693-578-7

VICTOR BOOKS
A division of SP Publications, Inc.
Wheaton, Illinois 60187

# CONTENTS

*for my primary accountability network*

David Ashworth

Rick Clyde

Ben Foulk

Ken Love

Rob Nicholson

Alan Retzman

Daryl Smith

Don Spachman

Ivan Timm

Karl Wolfe

Greg Wood

Dean Ziegler

*For ten years, in an annual accountability marathon, we have shared an enormous spectrum of pleasure and pain. These men have taught me more than I could have possibly taught them, and they have proved the thesis of this book, that life is truly God's curriculum.*

# FOREWORD

This Spiritual Formation book is for the Christian who hears God's call to a devotional life, and wants to better serve Him in the challenges of every day. It draws on the richness of Christian spirituality through the centuries of church history, but with an application to the twentieth-century believer who is involved in society, rather than withdrawn from it.

Spiritual Formation blends the best of traditional discipleship concepts with the more reflective disciplines of an individual journey toward friendship with God. It is a lifestyle, not a program; a relationship rather than a system; a journey instead of a road map. It calls us into holy partnership with God for our spiritual development.

As you read this book, and then others in the series, I hope that you will receive much more than information. My prayer is that you will experience new levels of formation of your mind and heart, and find yourself drawn closer to Christ.

Steven Harper, General Editor
Associate Professor of Spiritual Formation
Asbury Theological Seminary

# PREFACE

This is a book about spiritual formation "on the go." Other authors in this series are leading us through time-honored paths to deep spirituality through holy habits and daily and seasonal acts of devotion which move us toward a more profound sense of God and His nearness.

However, all of us tend to reflect from time to time on the fact that "as we were going, we were healed!" We look back on major life experiences and see that the events, themselves, were the real curriculum for our spiritual transformation.

Spiritual formation is not optional. In his profound book, *Shaped by the Word*, Dr. Robert Mulholland makes the point that all of us, every day, are being formed. The only options are the kinds of forces that are shaping us. I speculate that as much as ninety percent of spiritual formation comes from processing our daily pilgrimage—the regular stuff of life.

Spiritual disciplines which disengage us from daily life may turn out for many of us to be artificial exercises. The power of any learning and shaping experience is directly proportional to its purposeful connection with our being and our doing.

This book describes some common life experiences which may turn out to be your major freeways to the higher ground of your spiritual pilgrimage. Walk on, then, and embrace God's curriculum wrapped in grace for you!

Donald M. Joy
Asbury Theological Seminary
Wilmore, Kentucky 40390
1988

# ONE

## WALKING IN LIGHT

I was just concluding a trail-briefing session with students headed out for fourteen nights of sleeping on the forest floor in the Red River Gorge. We would be working with thirty high school people, including three juvenile offenders whose district judge had offered to accompany them on my camping adventure. I offer a course, Discipleship Development through Trail Camping. Students who elect the course see themselves in education and evangelism ministry and are ready to use the outdoor setting to win teens to Jesus.

As I was winding up the session, Doug smiled at me skeptically. He told me later that he did not believe me. What I had said was this, "I ask you to speak no religious words, to use no strategies to convert them to Christian faith. Live with them. Check their sore feet. Monitor their environment until they know they are safe, and that you will not allow anyone to take advantage of them. If you practice any daily devotional routine at home, do it in the woods. If you don't do daily religious discipline at home, don't fake it to impress the kids. They can see right through you. I predict that by Wednesday we will see our first conversion, on the kid's own initiative. By Friday evening's communion service, we will close the deal for Jesus with virtually every kid."

On Wednesday evening of our forest adventure, with our chuck wagon set up at Parched Corn Overlook near the Angel Windows Arches, I was sitting alone against a large ore-laced sandstone. Doug came out of the woods and headed toward the food preparation center. I saw him grin as he approached. This time he was wagging his head.

"I didn't believe you."

"About what?"

"Conversions without using the verbal approach. And yet, it just happened. You know Jim, one of the probationers with Judge Palmer? He just came to me and said he wanted to know how to get his life together, like some of us seem to have done. I could not believe what he had figured out about what was involved in being a Christian—just by being with us for four days! And he was so ripe. So ready! How did you know it would happen on Wednesday?"

"No magic. I have just watched it happen for nearly ten years. When we follow our rules, it always happens on the fourth day. It takes three days to unhook all of us from our culture and our addictions. Top quality diet, strenuous walking, a little suffering, and a sense each day that we are going somewhere in particular—on a map they have studied—that's the curriculum. Put three solid chunks of Jesus in any group of five teens and you can count on it. Everybody wants to be wholly alive!"

I have a simple thesis—that life itself is God's best curriculum for us. If we would be transformed into the likeness of God through Jesus, it is more likely to happen in daily life than anywhere else. For it is there that we confront issues needing a deep integrity grounded in Jesus. He is truly the center of all reality, the pot of gold at the end of all rainbows arched over those life storms formed from fear, distress, pain, tragedy, even doubt.

It is popular these days to "sell all and follow the cult leader." This takes the form of pursuing the "big events." But it also takes the form of adoring the distant guru, supporting a special "ministry," and believing that God will give you what you want if you obey the call of the cult hero by proving you have "seed faith" as you send him your money.

There is a much older tradition which suggests that we abandon our life vocation and pursue holiness through meditation, disciplines of reading, prayer, and specific attention to thinking holy thoughts and being holy. It is clear that Jesus knew the Scriptures and quoted them. But His call to discipleship does not demand obligations to literature, even the sacred Bible.

Jesus was a man of prayer and often retreated to be alone while He prayed. Yet He offered no formula or suggestion about how many minutes or hours each day one should pray. Indeed, He seemed to abhor the Pharisees' preoccupation with doing holy things by the clock. Jesus' call to obedience, now, in the present circumstance, is always a matter of subjecting one's motivation and speech and action to God's judgment of righteousness.

In this book I want to let you look at community—the need for faith to be nurtured in the company of other people. And I want you to support the traditional spiritual disciplines. But I will ask you to consider that the path to righteousness is not as simple as either the popular or the traditional approaches have seemed to offer.

On the one hand, the way Jesus calls us to take is the most difficult of all, because there is no escape from daily life, duty, and vocation. On the other, the way Jesus calls may affirm some deep intuitive sense you have had all along—that to be spiritually minded somehow has more to do with being the right kind of person than with doing the right things. And there's the rub. The burden of responsibility falls on us to keep our plows in the ground of daily living. If faith is going to work, it must work on the job, in the care of our children, and in the midst of conflict with spouse, family, or colleagues in the workplace.

## AN APPETITE FOR GOD

The backpacking story underscores a mystery I cannot fully explain. Stated most simply, it is this: All humans have an inner hunger for what is true, wholesome, and favors life. Right now, you are following that inner hunger. This means that you are capable of pursuing your appetite for God and holiness. Put that together with the thesis of this book—that daily life is God's main curriculum to bring us to holiness and wholeness—and you have a remarkably hopeful combination. It boils down to this: Wherever you find people, God is already at work. And God is active in all kinds of environments to make each of us a "thing alive" to Him, and reflecting the image of His Son Jesus. We often want to remove people from their environment, to take them to a meeting or seminar and complicate their lives by crowding their schedules with more and more religious activities. But Jesus most often wants to send us right back into our own circumstances and our own homes to let righteousness do its work there.

## LIGHT, LIFE, AND RIGHTEOUSNESS

Jesus made several "picture image" statements about Himself. "I am the light of the world. . . . I have come that you may have life and have it to the full. . . . Give them the full measure of My joy." These are end goals of Jesus. In the Beatitudes, Jesus describes the kind of people God does everything for. They are not the folks who are enjoying light, life, and joy. Instead, they are the poor, the grieving, and those trampled down by life's circumstances until they are tamed like a harnessed but as yet undisciplined domestic animal. In the first three Beatitudes, look at the groups and at what they receive.

The poor—the kingdom of heaven.

Those who grieve—comfort.

Those who are oppressed—the earth.

There is a sense in which the Beatitudes may be a ladder that we all have to climb, each step one at a time. Look at the conditions in the first three Beatitudes. Notice that each new one seems to grow out of the previous Beatitude's critical issue. For example, if I am starving to death, I have no proper sense of loss or grief over my own or another's anguish or death. And if I am locked into grief, and cannot respond to the iron hand of oppression, I simply collapse. But if I have come to terms with my poverty, I can learn to grieve, and later to shoulder up under the pain and suffering of external constraint, even abuse.

This pattern may be seen to move on up through the eight Beatitudes. But for now look only at the first three, and watch the change in demand come in the fourth.

Step four: Blessed are those who hunger
   and thirst for righteousness.
Step three: Blessed are the restrained/ meek.
Step two: Blessed are those who mourn.
Step one: Blessed are the poor.

While in the first three, the people trapped there need to do nothing except to wrestle with the experience of life's crucible to receive the promised attention which God provides, the fourth step is quite different. For the first time, it becomes critical for the individual to actively generate hunger and thirst, for it is the person in pursuit of righteousness who "shall be filled."

Let's look further at the first three Beatitudes as a ladder, and imagine what our "daily experience curriculum" might be.

 †    Poverty. "Blessed are the poor in spirit, for theirs is the kingdom of heaven." Jesus wrote this curriculum for all of us. It is easy to see how little power young children have in the world. They are poor in every sense—strength, influence, financial leverage. Their only resources are external to themselves. Jesus once said, "How hardly shall they that have riches come

"into the kingdom of God" (Mark 10:23, KJV). "Into the kingdom of God" literally means "under the Lordship of God." It is
not that rich people are bad, but that they are so almighty
independent! But poor people, like the sparrows, can more easily acknowledge that they belong only to God, and that if He
doesn't feed them, they die.

As adults, we sense our poverty when we have to ask for
help. Both our pride and our cleverness keep us from telling the
truth about our needs. We fake it when we cannot remember an
old schoolmate's name. We could have admitted our poverty
and said, "Help me with your name." We walk away congratu-
lating ourselves on covering our ignorance, but at heart we
know we were proud and deceitful and are going away diminished in some important way.

As we turn toward God, we will either fake it and pretend to be hot stuff, able to mouth the right words, or we tell
the truth. If we tell the truth, we confess our poverty, helplessness, and dependence on God. "Help!" is the first cry of every
Christian. It is easy to see why most Christians make their
decision for Jesus in childhood, adolescence, or young adult
trouble. Old habits of pride and independence are hard to
break, but not impossible.

† Grief. "Blessed are those who mourn, for they will be
comforted." How are the mourners blessed? It is interesting to
note that in the first three Beatitudes, no action is required, only
a condition. Grief is heavy because it is made up of the dark
reality of dealing with a major loss. It is a time for taking stock
of what will never be again. Children grieve over a lost afternoon of play. Teens grieve for friends lost when Dad's job
moves them across country. Young adults grieve over the failure
of an important relationship, a blown-up romance, a lost innocence. Grieving people are immobilized and rarely make it to
church. The opportunities for grief are everywhere. Today we
are urged to take valium or a little alcohol to cushion our in-

tense grief. We take our friends to the doctor to get something to see them through the funeral. The way of life that nurtures grief, that takes losses seriously and processes them straight, is not popular.

When Brent confided that he had been to the doctor because his girlfriend had broken up with him the previous Sunday, I asked why.

"To get some medicine, so I could keep my mind on my work."

"Brent, Jesus took His pain straight. On the cross, they offered Him a sedative, but when He tasted it and recognized that it was simply offered to kill His pain, He refused to drink it. I don't think you need tranquilizers to deal with your pain. Go ahead and cry. Treasure each deep feeling. It is the stuff which will make you gentle and kind. Don't kill the curriculum that comes with the territory when you are eighteen and a man of integrity."

It is not hard to see how a season of grief might become an important part of our life pilgrimage, even though we work hard to avoid incurring losses. Remember my thesis—all of life is God's curriculum, and grace and peace can work through any experience if we resolve to commit ourselves to obedience to Jesus.

†    Constraint. "Blessed are the meek, for they will inherit the earth." The word *meek* pictures someone who is harnessed to an inescapable load that was never wanted, but is painfully present and real. Children who are loved are tamed and civilized by parent-imposed duty. Meekness is having to brush your teeth and make your bed. Meekness is having to plan your own weekly junior high budget and give account for every penny of money entrusted to you.

Such constraint through accountability is something we think we can slough off when we become adults. If we are lucky we meet it in the Marines, or in the college years in an environment where we are offered a covenant and the modest supervision to remind us of our promises. Some of us find our first meekness test in the workplace when we must perform without complaint under circumstances that are painful, even humiliating. We make promises on our wedding day, and often long before, which limit our freedom in covenant ways which make for filling up the cup of meekness. All of us know that if Jesus gets hold of us, His discipline comes on line and continues to unfold in deeper and deeper rigor as long as we live. It is a cheap shot approach to spiritual formation which suggests that our spirituality is "out there," somewhere else, or is in doing religious things when we get home, or on our lunch break. The deepest formation of all is occurring while we are sweating in the crucible, as our wills are being tested and we are being ripened into wiser and gentler people by life's experiences.

So there they are, the three steps in the ladder before we reach the hunger and thirst for righteousness. The typical walk of life carries us through poverty, into grief, and sustains us in the tough days of tormenting discipline or abuse by life situations. Most of us find ourselves repeating cycles of pain and helplessness throughout life. Indeed, unless we meet sudden cataclysmic death, we are certain to discover helplessness, poverty of incapacity, grief of lost powers, and the discipline of disability. God's curriculum of life is dynamic and useful, but often unpredictable and cyclical in its patterns.

You can see that we were bringing off a developmental miracle with the backpackers—we were speeding up the poverty/grief/discipline sequence. We were also counting on using the curriculum of withdrawal from cultural luxuries—a kind of induced poverty. We were quite sure of the natural curriculum of sore feet and trail stress and discipline—some of it the discipline of keeping up and saving face within the peer group. We were simply providing a support environment in which the hunger for righteousness, truth, and holiness could awaken quickly.

Under the rigors of a thirty-pound pack, through poison ivy, among rattlesnakes and copperheads, in a compressed outdoor experience, far from telephones, radios, or television distractions, the hunger for righteousness, which God has planted deep in every human being, finally surfaces. We see that hunger, and the teens respond to Jesus' claims on their lives and are set free for life, light, and joy. What happens within them in the microcosm of a week in the back country camping experience, happens to us all in our own experiences across the years. We don't have to go into the forest to learn to hunger and thirst after righteousness.

## LIGHT OR DARKNESS?

In the First Epistle of John, some powerful pairs of opposites describe the life choices we are making. Three contrasts of action versus mere talking set the key life issues for us. Read chapter 1 from bottom to top to catch the significance of this ladder of choices.

10. If we say that we have not sinned we make Him a liar and His word is not in us.

9. If we *confess* our sins He is faithful and just to forgive us our sins, and to cleanse us from all unrighteousness.

8. If we say that we have no sin, we deceive ourselves, and the truth is not in us.

7. If we *walk* in the light as He is in the light, we have fellowship one with another, and the blood of Jesus Christ

His Son cleanseth us from all sin.

6. If we say that we have fellowship with Him, and walk in darkness, we lie and do not the truth.

5-4-3 God is light and in Him is no darkness at all. . . . We write unto you that your joy may be full. . . . that you also may *have fellowship* with us, and truly our fellowship is with the Father, and with His Son Jesus Christ.

It is clear that our behavior, our obedience, and our walk, are the true tests of our faith. Talk is cheap, and mere saying, perhaps mere cognitive consent, is in danger of turning out to be empty gesturing.

But notice the action words on the right-hand rungs—*confess, walk, have fellowship.* Like "hungering and thirsting after righteousness" in the Beatitudes, which is slowly developed by doing the homework of poverty, grief, and meekness, so here we must confess our sins, walk in the light, and stop all our meaningless and twisted talking, if we want to walk in continuing fellowship with one another, with God, and with Jesus Christ.

Set in the middle of these polar opposites is the choice—walk in light or walk in darkness. It is important that we choose to walk in the light and not in darkness. I do not want to leave you with the fallacy that you will inevitably become mature, holy, and profoundly transformed by God's grace if you simply endure life. Life experience is the curriculum, but we can flunk the final exam if we persistently walk in darkness and turn our life experiences into bitter dregs, resentment, and deformity.

Walking in light suggests perpetual honesty and integrity, and sticking close to people of truth and living with them in mutual respect. And in this passage, as elsewhere in Scripture, light nourishes life and stimulates growth. So we are well on the way to identifying the characteristics of the healthy person and the characteristics of the environment which nurtures life.

Walking in darkness suggests dishonesty and death, slinking around in shame and huddling with people of uncertain character. It means distrust, deception, and looking out for yourself, in an environment where everything decays and drifts into uncleanness.

## GET READY TO WALK!

Jesus' call to discipleship was consistently a call to obedience and action. He was not at home with abstractions. The three laws and four steps were not in His repertoire. Jesus relied on the primal, universal reality—act and be changed by your obedience. We have often tried the easier route of getting mental consent through checking beliefs.

I finished a Sunday morning sermon in a great college church many years ago and left the congregation hanging on the hook of Jesus' words, "You must be perfect, therefore, as your heavenly Father is perfect." Jesus had shown this holy life by a series of examples—that sarcasm and ridicule against your brother is the same as murder, that lusting after a person's sexual flesh is the same as adultery, that telling the truth needs no extravagant words, and that unconditional love works. The host pastor took the lectern and "finished my sermon" by essentially taking responsibility off his people for obeying Jesus in those calls to obedience in concrete action. We much prefer to explain away action by cognitive syllogism and abstract theory.

Dietrich Bonhoeffer put it tersely, "Only the one who obeys believes." This suggests that people who say they don't believe in God or wonder about the doctrine of the Incarnation or the Virgin Birth should first face questions about their obedience to God's commands and Jesus' call to "love God and love your neighbor as you love yourself." They will find that belief tends to follow behavior, but that mere belief rarely motivates behavior.

This suggests the major reason behind the colossal failure of efforts to educate us out of drunk driving, promiscuous sex, and gambling. We do not live out what we know. By past experience we are sure that we are exceptions. We have been drunk and gotten home safely. Since we cannot see the loss of thousands of brain cells for every ounce of alcohol consumed, we think we have beaten the system, unaware that we lose our ability to think as we play that game. We may have played the field sexually or played the horses gambling and claimed, "It didn't affect me." So long as we can walk away from the scene of failure, we think we have beaten the system. It is only the painful step of obedience, with or without feeling or conviction, that turns our self-centered selfishness around. Discipleship begins only with obedience.

## LIFE AS PILGRIMAGE

In this chapter, I have wanted you to become accustomed to looking at your life experience—your "walk." Jesus, who could have had any classroom on earth, chose to walk with the disciples for three years and to experience life with them. We learn and we are formed as we walk.

We choose whether we will obey Jesus and walk in the light. If we choose to hide our secret sins and our fears, we have rejected the one Person who *is* truth and life and light, and so we have chosen the opposite. We are on a negative adventure into denial of truth, life, and light, and are pursuing their opposites—deception, death, and darkness. But we are walking. And our formation is occurring as we are in process.

But if we choose to walk in honesty and fidelity, and are keeping current in our sense of responsibility and in expressions of respect, we will find that walking in the light as Jesus is in the light gives us fellowship with one another and with God and with Jesus who is light. There isn't much more to human existence that anyone could want!

# W HO?

If we walk in the light, as He is in the light, we
have fellowship with one another, and the
blood of Jesus, His Son, purifies us from every
sin.                                         1 John 1:7

## WHERE?

On a sheet of paper, draw a horizontal line. Label the left end
*birth* and the right end with your present age. Place asterisks at
points and ages which represent major Christian commitment
events. See your pilgrimage?

## WHAT?

Look at your calendar for next week and circle those appoint-
ments which are likely to move you toward deeper honesty and
integrity. Underline those which may make you vulnerable to
things which are not true, constructive, or oriented to light.
How can you take light into the dark moments of this week?

## WHY?

Your instinctual habits of punctuality and integrity are the fruit
of past promises and discipline. How will this week's light-and-
darkness choices affect future values and patterns?

## WHEN?

Can you postpone the integrity walk? At what cost? If you drift
into merely "saying" Christian words, can you risk the eternal
consequences?

# T W O

## EMERGING THROUGH LOVE

Joe grew up on Wooster Road, half a mile east of our home. He sprouted wings on a ten-speed bike when he turned twelve, and as I would pull alongside him on a summer day, in our little Morris Minor, he would call out to me, "How fast am I going?" So I would clock him as he made a burst of speed and encourage him along by calling, "Almost thirty miles an hour!"

By the time Joe turned fifteen he was more than six feet. Then the news broke. Joe was arrested for stealing a car which he and an accomplice then wrecked near Fort Wayne. He was sentenced to the Indiana Reformatory in Pendelton, and I didn't see Joe for a couple of years. When I ran into him on the street one Saturday afternoon near Hull House in Warsaw, I stopped, took his hand and didn't let go until I had extracted a promise that he would stop by to see me.

"I'll be there at eight tonight."

When he arrived, I scooped two dishes of ice cream and sat down across our kitchen table from Joe. "What was going on? I can't imagine you stealing a car."

"See, Steve and I are both adopted, and we were both born up in the Boston area. So we got this crazy idea that we ought to go and find out who we really are—you know—what kind of natural parents we really had and why they got rid of us."

I was learning things. I knew Joe went by the name of the family down the road from us, but his story was much more complicated than that. His legal name was different from our neighbor's name, and his birth identity was still something else, and he didn't have a clue who his natural parents were.

"What did you plan to do when you got to Boston?"

"Well, see, I know the county I was born in, but the adoption agency wouldn't tell me my real mother's name or anything like that. So, I had this idea I would walk into the courthouse and demand to know who I really am. I guess I thought I could find out somehow."

"Then what?"

"I just wanted to track down my mom. I knew she used to work in a bar, so I supposed she still did. If I could find her, I just wanted to walk in on her and say, 'Hi! I'm your kid!' How do you like that?"

"That sounds right," I said, pondering a reality I had never even considered. "Then what?"

"Well, I would have asked her about who my real daddy was, and I would have tracked him down, but I didn't want to see him or talk to him or anything like that."

"Why did you want to know about him then?"

"I just wanted to track him down, you know, and stand outside his house and throw rocks through his windows all night long."

I was numb. I had no capacity to respond to Joe on this one. But it gave me a signal that we worked on for a couple of hours that evening, and then continued off and on for the next ten years. Joe suffered not only from natural-father abandonment and irresponsibility. He suffered also because his adoptive father abandoned him and his adoptive mother. Her second husband, my neighbor Ed, completely rejected Joe.

Contrast this story with an episode in our granddaughter Heather's life. When Heather was in first grade, Mike, her dad, invited her to help him clean the house one Saturday. Justin and Lesli, a baby and a five-year-old sister, were too young to help.

Something really clicked in Heather. She sensed that she had power over any household clutter and disorder, and she began to systematically clean the house, including vacuuming every morning before the other family members were up and about. Then, after school when Heather would come through the door, she would take one quick walk around the house to see how it looked after a day of living in it. Occasionally she would scold Lesli, "I had it all clean this morning and you messed everything up."

At first the family thought it was astonishing and cute, and Heather got a lot of affirmation. Then, one evening at bedtime, her daddy sat her on his lap. "Heather, honey, you are a little girl and you don't need to clean the house every day or worry about keeping it neat. We will do that, and sometimes you can help, but it is not your responsibility. It is mine and it is Mommy's, but you are not supposed to feel you have to clean the house and worry about keeping it straight."

Let these two stories set the stage for thinking about the very earliest steps in our lifelong pilgrimage. Our primary family relationships provide the most far-reaching impact on our spiritual formation. These life experiences are powerful partly because they are our earliest ones. But they are powerful also because they are persistent; we invest more time in our primary family relationships than we do in most others. When we marry, we spend more time with spouse and our own children, but those are relationships which simply extend the original family experiences. Parents represent God's first curriculum, the images of God surrounding every baby's birth.

In this chapter we need to look at those first steps in the life journey—steps so long ago and so bereft of language that we have few tools of thought to even recall their importance. Yet those very earliest relationships deeply affect our pilgrimage of faith.

## GOD HAS PLACED THE SOLITARY IN FAMILIES

Humans do not thrive when they are isolated. "Solitary confinement" is a most troublesome penalty, whether in prison or in the home. "It is not good that Adam should remain alone" is God's word about the human need for community. In the Creation document God's statement sets the stage for "splitting the Adam" into female and male so as to begin with a microcosm community; we still look to marriage and the family as the bottom line. People deserve to be loved, affirmed, and regularly recharged for moving out into a lonely world. Let's look at the critical support features which the family provides.

† Conception. Before any new life begins, there is human touch, sexual intimacy, and an instinctual gesturing of affection. Nobody gets born—except by in vitro fertilization or by artificial insemination—unless two people who form a community of affection actually rehearse the lifelong promise of support and affirmation. There are, of course, fraudulent parents whose pregnancies were accidents which occurred as they gestured exploitation or even abuse in the sexual arena. Some of these people are tamed by the nine months of reflection and preparation for caring for a new life. Others simply further insulate themselves against responsibility and bring themselves and the rest of us more and more grief.

It was the magic of conception and the creation of new life which inspired the Psalmist to sing:

You created my inmost being;
You knit me together in my mother's womb.
I praise You because I am fearfully and wonderfully made;
Your works are wonderful,
I know that full well.
My frame was not hidden from You

# EMERGING THROUGH LOVE

When I was made in the secret place.
When I was woven together in the depths of the earth,
Your eyes saw my unformed body. . . .

Psalm 139:13-15

† Prenatal memory. Conception sets the stage for the beginning of life. A heartbeat can be detected as early as the second month. A baby has fingernails as early as the twelfth week, and responds to sounds in the outer world and to the mother's movement for several months before delivery. Amazing stories are being told about prenatal memory and learning. One conductor reported that as he led an orchestra through the first reading of a classical work, he was amazed that he was anticipating correctly the cello line even before he turned the page. When he reported this at a family gathering, his mother, a cellist, laughed and told him she had worked persistently on mastering her part of that very work late during her pregnancy with him. He had evidently tucked that musical pattern away in deep memory for more than forty years.

† Birth. An absolute wonder of the late twentieth century is that we are now witnessing the priority of bringing both mother and father into the world of the child immediately at birth. One family reported to me that their "afterthought child," a girl, was born after the parents had been through a seminar in which I reported the amazing news about opportunities for birth bonding. They took their three sons, one already in his teens, into the birthing room. I watched this family for three days recently at a family camp and was struck by the way these young men, now ranging from twelve to seventeen, were taking care of a four-year-old girl. The mother told me that she and her husband had experimented with my teaching, with amazing results.

"People ask me what I pay my sons to sit with the family in church and to help with the care of our daughter. Nobody else has teenagers—boys or girls—who help out like our sons do. They frequently ask, 'Isn't it my turn to take care of Annie?' "

† Lifelong love. The magic of the first two-and-one-half hours of life, with the deep memories of security, acceptance, and affirmation which are telegraphed to the child by touch, and sound are only a sample of the long-term love that the child will receive from the parents. But it appears that the parents too are changed by the birth-bonding process and, indeed, find themselves generating long-term feelings of closeness and attachment stimulated by the abundant touch and total contact of the first few hours after the baby's birth. Child abuse, for example, is more often directed toward a child who was separated from the mother by medical problems immediately at birth than toward a child who was early bonded to the mother. I believe that as more fathers take an active part in the birthing experience, the more typically harsh male responses toward children may be mellowed.

Early intimacy predicts long-term intimate commitment to children. Hugs, kisses, and affirmation are the parents' major emotional gift to children. How easy it is to become negative coaches, harping on the child's mistakes, clumsiness, and incompetence at adult tasks, as measured by adult standards. Such ventilation of parental anger and impatience is a major source of the destruction of the child's sense of self-worth. Bonding is a lifelong agenda. Rituals of saying good-bye and hello with touch and embrace are minimum positive blocks as we build the interior castle of a child's sense of self.

## *GOD'S FIRST CURRICULUM*

God has given us all that we need to know of Himself in Jesus, in the Incarnation by which God became "flesh and dwelt among us." However, this knowledge does not come first in our experience, for parents are God's first curriculum for the young child. God created humans in the image or likeness of God. However deformed that image may be by sin, God's imprint remains. Human difference from the animals is not primarily in our physical characteristics, but in being created as moral and spiritual beings.

There is a sense in which any mother and any father, as they set about to create new life, are operating on a charter issued by God in His Creation. That charter grants them the rights and responsibilities of being co-creators with Him, and of thereafter representing God to the child. Everything that is true, righteous, just, and good should be held out so that the child learns to love truth, to hunger for righteousness and justice, and to search always for the good. Parenting, then, is a contract to teach in God's university. No one can shift from that responsibility simply because they "do not believe in God." It is a universal obligation and comes with the territory of co-creating new life.

In the process, God mellows up people who have any remaining trace of love for truth and beauty. At the sight of a new baby, parents are often struck dumb. "We couldn't have *done* this!" they exclaim. Life and birth are miracles that bring God near in tangible form. The child is indeed a "bundle from heaven," and God will use instinctual parental fidelity to build images of trust to establish the foundations for faith. God's curriculum is not very religious looking, and holds some surprises for all of us.

Children all come with a built-in magnet for God, for truth, righteousness, justice, and what is good. If parents offer basic affirmation and a safe environment, the child will be formed in an innocence they themselves cannot imagine—because their own innocence has so long been silenced by the guilt of their present adult irresponsibilities. Ironically, the child often becomes God's second curriculum for parents as they see

God represented in their little one.

Mothers are given special "image of God" gifts which run toward *encompassing love,* the unconditional attachment and love which is like God's love and expressed by the Hebrew word *kesed.* Encompassing love is visible in the gestures of a mother who cradles the baby to herself closely. The motor of that affection seems to be the built-in desire to absorb the baby back into the self from which it was formed, almost literally hugging it to the center of the torso. But the motor is called "mother love," because it always seeks to protect and comfort the child. This instinctual, motherly encompassing gesture, expressed in a thousand other parallel transactions with the baby, is the curriculum by which her child will understand the everlasting, unconditional love of God, and will be prepared to enter into community, to trust, and to experience God in the community. Israel was the bride, and the church is the body of Christ, and His bride. Both suggest the intimate, steadfast and loving God, and mothers have an edge on representing that part of the image of God.

Fathers seem specially to have a deposit of "image of God" gifts which run toward *engrossing love,* and an objective sense of righteousness and justice. God is described in both Testaments as loving justice and mercy. A father guides the child "with his eye," celebrates autonomy, and urges the child's readiness to engage responsibility and freedom. We see a father's encompassing love in the gestures he makes. Instead of the nestling hug, a father is more often seen dandling a child in what the mothers think are precarious positions. He holds the little feet to his beltline and engrosses the baby face to face. Then he swings, dangles from a knee, even tosses the child in the air. Mother sometimes cringes, but Father has a built-in curriculum by which the child will experience the "wholly other" Daddy, in preparation for contemplating the "wholly other" Father-God.

The child's continuing contact with both a father and a mother, then, expands God's first curriculum, as the child is formed in maturity and responsibility.

## FORMATION IN COMMUNITY

The healthiest place to grow up is in an intergenerational family, rich in grandparents, aunts, uncles, and cousins. Of course, if the family is deformed there may be deformity for sale, but healthy intergenerational families are a superb environment in which to be formed in the image of God. Let's consider some of the benefits.

† Stimulation. Humans need to talk and to be talked to. There is a direct correlation between level of stimulation and measured intelligence; children who live in environments rich in verbal stimulation come out with higher scores. For infants especially, touch boosts health and develops the magnet for being friendly as an adult. Children raised alone may lack the social skills and personal warmth so often evident in adults who have been reared in larger and richer family environments.

† Multiple models. As the growing child magnetically turns to the respected father and mother to "take a measure" of what it is going to mean to be a man or to be a woman, the lucky kid has backup models in older brothers or sisters, aunts or uncles, and grandparents. There is some speculation that grandparents may have stronger magnetic appeal to children than we have thought. Many people cite their grandparents as the most influential factor in bringing them to faith. Either way, the important thing is that a whole string of witnesses to sex roles, sexual identity, and faith values and beliefs become powerful levers to move the child toward maturity and toward faith.

† Confrontation. One of the most urgent needs all of us have is to test our ideas on respected people. "Sometimes I have to get you angry to know what you really believe," one of our

sons told us at seventeen. "Thanks alot," I responded.

Casual friends rarely confront us, and if we do not have a kinship or surrogate network of at least twenty people, we could move through life without accountability to anybody, without testing our ideas and values against intergenerational kin and wise people, and without awareness that other points of view must be taken into account in the real world. We need people in order to become human and to be pushed to our very best.

† Kinship system. Healthy people have been nurtured in a high-commitment kinship system. If it is true that we need a minimum of about twenty people with whom we maintain strong connections, it will be important to nurture these surrogate family friendships across a lifetime. As we move into adulthood, we tend to handpick our support network family. E. Mansell Pattison, distinguished Christian psychiatrist, notes that healthy adults he has observed tend to draw about one-half of their base of twenty people from family members—rather evenly divided between immediate relatives and those at the uncle, aunt, cousin, and grandparent level. He says that we pick up about one-fourth from workplace contacts, including church and clubs; the other one-fourth is a lifelong collection.

I have called this group our "hand-held trampoline." These are people who let us jump and scream for joy and who also hang on when we suffer. These are people who are important to us, with whom we have frequent face-to-face contact, and in whom we have a high emotional investment. Beyond this, the acid test of relationship hinges on whether they would put their money at risk if we were desperate. Would they stick with us?

You can see how such a community network provides a healthy perspective in which we regularly and intimately exchange perspectives and sharpen each other's sanity.

Jesus was intent on creating a new community. First it

was a group of twelve, then one hundred twenty, and then five thousand; always His focus seemed to be on community for spiritual development, health, and wholeness. "Where two or three of you have gathered, there I am in the midst," He said.

Indeed, the concept of the church as Jesus' body is imaged as a community. Both Jesus and Paul used *head* and *body* as metaphors of intimacy and mutual interdependency. Though *head* has been distorted by some people to suggest position and power, it is consistently used in Scripture to denote absolute dependency on the body, and on the "two becoming one" in the marriage symbolism.

The Trinity exists coeternal as community. Genesis 1 exclaims for the Trinity, "Let Us create. . . . in Our image"! And Jesus, in words in John 17, notes the interdependence between Himself and the Father, and invites us all into community that we may be one with Him and the Father, and that the world may know that God sent Jesus.

If families are competitive, chaotic, or artificial "showcase" kinds of families, they seriously misrepresent God's image and can deform our understanding of the Trinity in the process. But when families are faithful, respect-based, and celebrating communities of decision, action, and witness, then the image of God appears in faithfulness, nurturing our spiritual formation. The same test must be put on our support networks, because it is easy to pursue friendships out of self-interest, out of our need for power or prestige, or even our need to control other people. So, throughout life, we are building a model of the Trinity and are projecting image-of-God impressions simply by being Christians in community.

## *BARRIERS TO COMMUNITY*

Three problem areas surface as we look at ways of nurturing positive community relationships—our mobility, our health, and our aging.

† Mobility. Living as we do in a technological society which requires major upheavals on an average of once in four years, many people find themselves just recovering from the grief of lost networks when yet another move is announced. These high-mobility people suffer more clinical grief than those who remain well rooted in the same geographical community year after year. The grief is commonly expressed as a nagging depression which occurs within a few weeks of arrival in a new place.

We tend to ignore or trivialize grief in our children when we uproot them and urge them to "go out and make new friends." What we hope is that they will forget about their old friends back in the other community. We might more wisely urge them to write a letter or to make a phone call to describe their new setting to friends they have left behind. The new community will eventually take root in their emotions in direct proportion to their newly forming network. Busy executives and homemakers frequently remain impoverished longer than their children, some of them denying the grief and turning to alcohol or drugs to mask the hollow feelings which surround their losses. It is not infrequent that stress-related illnesses emerge within the family, when moves are frequent and networking is limited to a few years at best.

† Health. We need our networks most when things are not going well. When illness, disease, or depression strikes, people are a primary prescription for bringing us back to health. There is an amazing irony here. When we are ill, we are cultur- ally conditioned to protest, "I don't want anyone to see me like this." That unhealthy conclusion is, sadly, matched by our ten- dency to say about others, "I don't know what to say, so I'll just send over a card and a hot dish and leave it at the door." But it is the look and the touch that give health and life.

Linda's doctor told her, "You will be here in the Hope

Center for twelve weeks of chemotherapy. You have T-cell lymphoma. I want to have someone scheduled to stay with you every day for that time. You can book different people, but you must not be alone."

"I was horrified. I worried that the doctor thought I might croak any day during therapy," Linda gasped. "But she simply knew I needed to keep talking as I underwent the therapy and had to deal with all of the effects. So, bless their hearts, four of my friends agreed to rotate a week with me once a month to see me through this."

Depressive or suicidal patients want to be alone. "You will only hurt me if you tell anyone what I'm going to do," one distraught man told me. Yet his telling me was itself a cry for help; left alone, he was only going to deteriorate further. People out of touch with others become disoriented. Their humanity is somehow diminished when a support system is not working for them.

  † Aging. As our support network is diminished by the death of those we love, disorientation, depression, and isolation become predictable. People whose network begins to slip tend to become so critical in their needs that some of us are frightened away—only to further complicate their aloneness. Isolated people are not going to get well, simply by being booked for private therapy sessions. It is community which gives them perspective and health.

## LIVING IN COMMUNITY

In this chapter I have wanted you to see the giant brushstrokes from Creation, in which God seems to have announced, "It is not good that humans should be alone; I will create community for them." This motif is written into history and God's ways with His people. It is written into the incarnation of God in Jesus who came to walk with us, to live out His life in community with us, to form us into faith communities, and to promise to meet personally when two or three of us gather in His name.

I have asked you to look at the family as "God's first curriculum" in disclosing His image to each human being from birth onward. And we have concluded by looking at ways of establishing and sustaining significant relationships in our network systems, seeing them as an important "trampoline" to sustain the shocks of our life, as we walk on day by day, living out our vocation as men and women obedient to Jesus.

It is in this sense that our discipleship is likely being hammered out in the crucible of daily life, as we learn what it means to be committed to the health and welfare of other people, and also to accept support from others when we are inclined to move into isolation.

# WHO?

It is not good for _____
to be alone.                Genesis 2:18

## WHERE?

Write your name on the line above. Then look at the timeline you began in chapter 1. Think of this as your pilgrimage or life map. Block off your first ten years and list some very significant people along the line. Why are they there?

## WHAT?

Plan this week to make contact with at least two people from your first ten years of life. Now list three youngsters who are important to you. For each, draw a life map as you did for yourself and list the important people on whom they are depending, or might come to depend, if you intervened.

## WHY?

Pause to reflect and to doodle in your journal or in the margin here. Ask God, "Why did You create the family? What do You intend to do about families that fall apart and about children who lose a parent in the early critical years? What do You have in mind for abandoned, abused, and rejected children?"

## WHEN?

Spend a few minutes in thanksgiving to God for surrounding you for good and for giving you His first curriculum in the critical years.

# THREE

## WRESTLING WITH IDENTITY

When Pearl Harbor was attacked on December 7, 1941, I was just thirteen, but already six feet tall, and quite sure of who I was and what I was becoming. While I was growing up, my mother's extended family was almost all a thousand miles away in Indiana, but my father's family lived nearby. Dad had four surviving brothers. We had buried Irvin at the age of twenty-nine, after he drowned in a fishing accident. My four uncles were models, mentors, and affirming friends, as I explored the idea of what it was to be a Joy growing up in rural Kansas. Dad's two younger sisters, Mary and Ellen Mae, were also important to me. They had played childhood "mothers" to me, since I was the first grandchild in the expanding Joy clan. Mary lived with us and was like an older sister, riding the school bus every day to high school as I started first grade.

By 1941 those important aunts had fallen in love and were married to young Christian stalwarts who happened also to be brothers and devout Quakers. And when the draft whisked away every other able-bodied young man, my new uncles stayed. They were conscientious objectors, and World War II was not a time when such objection was widely heard of, much less respected. As I moved into the high school years, I was an easy target for some macho peers who scapegoated me with the CO label. It clung to me like rotten eggs and was accompanied by minor physical harassment. The label persisted through three years of high school.

I suppose that at some level the agony of those years was positive for me, though I would never choose to pass through such a crucible again or would I recommend it for anyone else.

I knew that God had a claim on my life, indeed, that He would not let me go without a vocation fully surrendered to be a minister. I also knew that there was no more loyal American than I. While I did not have any objection to military service for myself, I loved Ellen Mae and Mary and their bright new Quaker husbands, and supported their positions of conscience. I was embarrassed that the CO label was being scrambled to give God a bad name, since my commitment to Jesus was assumed by some of my friends to be a package deal with the conscientious objector position.

I left high school at the end of my junior year and applied for admission to the US Navy's fast-track V-12 officers training program. It was not enlistment into military service, but it opened the door for me to escape the personal holocaust of the Fowler High School and to be admitted into college as a certified student suitable for screening into the Navy's fast-track training school. At the peak of World War II, manpower was tight and the Navy had an eye on getting a few eighteen-year-olds with one year of college behind them.

If I had wanted really to impress my tormentors, I would have enlisted straight into military service in a wild effort to stop the scapegoating and name-calling. But I simply had to get on with my life. By the end of my freshman year at Central College, the shameful labels were far behind me, and the war had ended.

Ironically, twenty-four years later I would listen and pose the questions with a son who had to work through the CO option at the height of the Vietnam War. The boundaries which protect sons from their fathers' pain kept my horror story inside me, during 1971, as our son was turning eighteen.

# *IDENTITY QUESTIONS*

I have told this story simply to set the stage for looking at the trauma of identity formation, a major part of the curriculum on the path toward mature faith. My story, told here for the first time, remained my private crucible during those formative years. No doubt many people suffer the slings and arrows of insult, assault, scapegoating, and harassment in forms much more traumatic than my own. Those who manage to be spared the public humiliation still may be plagued by feelings of inferiority, of shame, and of incompetence. These universal feelings, now neatly labeled low self-esteem, guarantee that most of us have an identity agenda mixed with pain from our formative years. As you read this chapter, turn your memory back and let the grace of Jesus work through the years of wrestling with those deepest of all questions: Who am I? Why am I here? Where did I come from? Where am I going? Does anyone value me?

When we ask the identity questions, it is easy to imagine that we are reflecting twentieth-century psychology. I would have made that judgment until twenty years ago when I discovered a sentence in John's Gospel that preserves for us an identity profile of Jesus. The setting is the Upper Room, as Jesus was about to wash His disciples' feet.

> Jesus, knowing that the Father had given all things into His hands, and that He had come from God and was going to God, rose from supper, laid aside His garments, and girded Himself with a towel. Then He poured water into a basin and began to wash the disciples' feet, and to wipe them with the towel with which He was girded.
>
> John 13:3-5, RSV

Embedded in this complicated sentence are the three planks which form every person's sense of identity. Jesus knew why He was in the world—"the Father had given all things into His hands." Jesus knew where He came from, saw Himself in the perspective of history and present time—"He had come from God." And Jesus knew where He was going, had a sense of destiny—"He was going to God."

## WHY AM I HERE?

Jesus knew that the Father had put all things in His hands. The sense of vocation—knowing why we are in the world—confronts us almost from infancy. At first we imitate the big folks around us. We pick a "model" and try to copy the vocation of being grown up. Indeed, we are almost helplessly caught into imagining ourselves in the very job of that most important adult, normally the parent of the same sex. We imitate the visible behavior of the admired person, want to walk around in that person's shoes, affect their posture, gesture, and speech. Then, as our world blossoms into alternative models, we experiment in fantasy with other vocations. Most important is the vocation "to be a woman" or "to be a man," as defined in the microcosm of culture in which we are formed.

When I was fifteen, my voice teacher gave me sheet music for the song by Maude Louise Ray, "My Task." It matched closely the vision of radical Christian commitment I was picking up at home and at church. And "My Task" made vocation a bigger for me picture than a "life job." Look at the song's definitions of our task:

> To love someone more dearly ev'ry day,
> To help a wandering child to find his way,
> To ponder o'er a noble tho't and pray,
> And smile when evening falls,

> This is my task.
> To follow truth as blind men long for light,
> To do my best from dawn of day till night,
> To keep my heart fit for His holy sight,
> And answer when He calls,
> This is my task.¹

If we don't have a sense of vocation larger than *job*, we tend to lose our love of life and anticipation of each day. Life becomes monotonous and work seems like drudgery. Retirement looms like a death sentence—which it often is. The man or woman who fell in love with the job of being a mother or of sharpening a skill much in demand, and highly rewarded in salary and benefits, is just as likely to fall out of love with the prison of routine. Having a sense of vocation, of larger life meaning, sets us free even while we are locked into the cabin of the home or the cell of the workplace.

Vocation means a vision of meaning for one's life—the knowledge that "I have come to this planet for such a time, and I am thankful to be here and to be myself with the work I know is here for me to do." This vision offers us affirmation on a daily basis. Prayer, social contact, any human exchange becomes an occasion for celebration that "I am myself; I am here; I am where I belong." These are portable perspectives that help us to understand St. Paul's amazing statement, "I have learned to be content whatever the circumstances" (Philippians 4:11).

Without a sense of vocation larger than any particular job, restlessness, boredom, and depression tend to haunt the workplace. The unbelievable consumption of narcotics, street drugs, and alcohol by people on the job, or on the way home on a daily basis, suggests that a vision of vocation is missing and that work has become meaningless and draining. The drugs mask the true helplessness they feel in the absence of knowing what today means in the scheme of a lifetime.

With each shift of my several professional careers, for several months I have had to fall on my knees, normally in the dark hours of early morning as I arrived at my work area. "Help me to know who I am and who You are. Let me see why I am in this place today." These are important transition agendas. A similar searching pattern of prayer occurs whenever I pass through the valley or a trough of pain. My careers have not turned out to be what I thought God was calling me to, so I have had to work through the ambiguity by surrendering my vision in exchange for God's reinterpretation. My early pastoral or missionary call, it turns out, is a call to a more generic ministry, a people vocation. Whether I was a sophomore in college, a denominational executive, or a professor, my vocation has remained constant; only the career or job has shifted.

## WHERE DID I COME FROM?

At a literal, physical level, the question plagues the mind of every emerging adolescent. But the question has facets which begin to shine and to probe throughout a lifetime. Jesus knew that He had come from God. His origin was unique, to be sure; but coming to terms with His special genetic origin and His home of launching was likely as great a task for Him as for any of us. The issue is larger than the merely biological or sociological questions we might compose. Consider some of the questions:

† What are my obligations to my family?

† Where are my roots when it comes to beliefs and traditions?

† Am I locked into my own culture of origin?

† Is my purpose in life primarily obligated to "return" to my own people?

† Or am I called to reach out, to step out of my own family, my own culture, and to be useful in a new or even alien

environment?

†    What shall I do about my accumulated history—the reputation of my family?

†    Shall I own or deny my own past reputation?

†    Indeed, have I forfeited my vocation because I "blew off" my childhood or adolescent vision or dream?

These are only a few of the questions we face as we contemplate our sense of identity. And as adults, often at mid-life or in mid-career, we find a way to pick up the true vocation we were unable to embrace in our youth.

We are all daughters and sons of Adam and are therefore fallen. This indelible mark which has been passed onto the race out of original failure and sin may be as good a metaphor as any to account for a universal phenomenon—low self-esteem. Who has not gasped at some moment, "If they only knew who I really am, they would know I do not deserve this honor, this position, this privilege." This painful, often fleeting sensation, is a tremor at the root of the identity question, "Where did I come from?" Jeremiah cried out, "I am only a child." Moses objected, "I am no fluent man with speech." "Not me, Lord! Ask someone else," is often a cry rising out of deep feelings of inferiority.

One of the most intriguing discoveries of Jean Piaget, and a continuing legacy of his in that human development sphere known as *structuralism*, is the concept that humans are constantly reorganizing their life experiences through a process he called adaptation. They assimilate new experiences which, in turn, explode their old structures. And with the breakage of the inadequate boxes, a transformation occurs in which old understandings and facts are looked at again, organized in another way, and brought forward in an updated form. This process produces another phenomenon Piaget called *hierarchical integration*. And here is the miracle: nothing is ever lost, but everything is constantly being transformed, expanded, and refined. [2]

This means that a lost childhood or a wasted youth

need never be denied or pitched away out of shame. It can all be salvaged, put into perspective, and sanctified. Indeed, the tendency to deny, hide, or deceive is always rooted in the shame of original sin. The call for integrity is always a call to honesty, owning one's past, and giving it over to the transformation of grace. Today we are impoverished because so many good people in the churches have stonewalled their histories. We used to hear people's life stories in public testimonies, and young and old alike would celebrate the miracle of God's transforming grace. But today we are less likely to tell our stories and not at all likely to describe the trajectory of transformation. And never have so many troubled people needed more to hear how "hierarchical integration" has turned darkness into light, pain into promise, and grief into hope.

Imagine what a powerful treasure is the person who allows grace and honest reflection to work through a damaged childhood, sexual abuse or misfortune, or any other major loss. Joseph's sobbing response to his brothers who had abused him as a youth, "You meant it to me for evil, but God has provided grace to turn it into something good," is the cry of many ripened and wise Christians.

Wayne Alderson's "Value of the Person" training program is a product of his own tragedy and the horrors of surviving as a point man pushing into Nazi Germany. Indeed, his forehead carries an enormously gouged scar sustained when a grenade exploded at point-blank range, killing his best friend who took the direct explosion. Many people bury their tragedies, but Alderson has allowed God to make his loss flower into a program which transforms the industrial workplace and is saving companies from bankruptcy. His near loss of life itself has been transformed into a heightened sense of the value of every person. Once an aggressive, competitive leader, he is now an industrial evangelist on behalf of mutual respect, cooperation, and savoring the uniqueness of every person. [3]

To the question, "Where did I come from?" we must ask, then, "Who am I in time and space?" You can see that the issues blend into the prior question, "Why am I here?" And we are well on the way to sensing our own value and accepting our vocation of coming home to the truth. One generic meaning of repentance is that we accept where we have come from up to the present moment and own that history. We own our history when we stop hiding or denying parts of our lives. When we own our history, we embrace what really happened and find tools of thought and speech by which we are able to release the secrets to carefully trusted mentors or small support communities. When we are able to thus own our histories, Jesus can make us new and transform what is past.

## WHERE AM I GOING?

Daniel Levinson and his colleagues who have been studying the seasons of life[4] for both men and women have found that each "zero marker" point evokes an adjustment to life: the big twenty, the larger thirty, and the frightening forty, and the deadly fifty are followed of course by the unwelcome sixty, and more. By the age of forty, Levinson found in his men's sample, death begins to figure into the life vision. It looms significantly in their assessment of their successes or failures in achievement of early goals. By age fifty, death is almost literally breathing on men. Only a slim segment of his sample of men furnished positive life attitudes beyond fifty. Clearly the issue is, "Where am I going?" Levinson is heavily influenced by Erik Erikson whose "eight ages of man" speculative model of development struck the awesome polarity of "ego integrity versus despair" as the final stage of life.

We should not be surprised at Levinson's findings, perhaps. It is striking that he completely avoided taking data on the religious life of his sample of men. The omission may tell us a good deal about Levinson, and it may hide the dimension of men's lives which might have been the discriminator between men with more positive adjustments and those with a downturn in their general well-being because of pessimism. Any man or woman who has come to terms with the question, "Where am I going?" will have a sense of going back to God—that is, facing God at the end of earthly life. On a physical level, it is dust returning to dust. At the cosmic and faith level, it is a moving toward the ultimate reunion with the God-Creator-Redeemer who always regards life as gift, and death as an occasion for consummating glory and celebration.

Today's mature adults who are at peace with who they are, with their vocation and their origins, tend to take occasional inventory with a positive surge of satisfaction. "From here on in, everything else is a bonus," is a contented breath of such a person. To know that you are going back to God can usher in a season of life which is not driven by trying frantically to work yourself to death, to please a parent long dead, or to impress the historians. It is enough to know that you dare not try to "impress" your audience of one—God! He knows you, is unconditionally committed to your eternal good, and can see through your smallest deceptive games in that life adventure marked "success."

Realizing the transparent kind of life that opens up to those who find their full identity in the dimensions of John 13, it is plausible, finally, to see how Jesus could walk into Jerusalem and accept no sword or other protection from the crowds. Truth is ultimately ready to let happen what will. "I must go to Jerusalem!" Jesus reminded some advisors who cautioned it might be unsafe.

Not long ago I worked side by side with a man who lives and ministers in the troubled heart of a great city. "I have been marked for death," he told me quietly, as he described a pastoral intervention he had made for a man who was supposed to die in a gang-style murder, but who managed to stay alive. The pastor cannot allow himself to be held hostage by fear, by arming himself or his house. There is a remarkable peace in being strung on a line between "coming from God" and "going back to God." It means that everything in between belongs to God too.

To know that we are going back to God also keeps our personal integrity and motivation for vocation on course. If God is both the origin and the ultimate target, then God's character necessarily runs through the dreams, the energy, and the motivations that drive our daily work. So we can expect to have our own dreams and our schemes sanctified by the penetrating light of God's justice, truthfulness, and unconditional love.

## A QUESTION OF VALUE

All of us face the feelings of isolation. Chip sat in my office struggling with the hopes of his parents and the pull of his peers. "It's a tough choice," I said, when I had tested the strength of both ends of that tension as best he could describe them.

"I don't see why I can't have both." Chip shifted uncomfortably. It would mean deceiving his parents to keep them happy. What he wanted was the approval of his peers by continuing his destructive appetites of consumption with them.

Knowing how big the temptation was to try the old game, I said, "You likely can't have it both ways."

Jesus could not have it both ways either. He seems not to have had any illusions about making an impression on the established religious cultures, even the most conserving tradition of the Pharisees. Instead, He handpicked a few people, pretty ordinary ones, to whom to impart His vision. When you read Jesus' hopes as He calls the disciples His friends, and note that servants do not know their master's business, but friends do, you know that Jesus expected to be supported by a network of identity-confirming friends to the very end (John 15).

So, let's tell the truth. We simply must surround ourselves with solid people with whom we can carry on an honest dialogue. We need to look into their faces as we float our best and our worst news. We need to sense that we are not alone in the world.

Our first and likely the most significant network of support for such feedback on our identity and our worth is in our family members—father, mother, brothers and sisters. But by the middle of the second decade of life, we tend to look for a wider circle—our peers, among whom most of us locate one exclusive partner with whom we long to share our deepest and most unspeakable thoughts, hopes, and fears. And we are fortunate indeed if we can retain the support of family as we enlarge our "trampoline"[5] to include that handpicked cadre of support and trust.

But we have to accept the fact that any of us may come to the bottom line and discover that we must make a decision, lay down our career, or even our life, and do it alone. Jesus did, for He was abandoned by the three-year solidarity core group. If He had been a loner throughout the thirty-three years of His life, we could understand His isolation. But His social history is one of intimate family relationships and a magnetic association with a dozen men and a larger network of friends and acquaintances.

The ultimate loneliness of Jesus is heard in His dying wail, "My God, My God, why have You forsaken Me?" That cry represents an extreme isolation which none of us will ever match, but which all of us know to be a legitimate feeling. In our better moments when we cry, "Does anyone value me?" we will be able to say yes, and to name the names of people who unconditionally support and treasure us, or to go in search of ways of becoming and of finding others who are able to support people profoundly.

## *FINDING WHO YOU REALLY ARE*

As you look at the basic questions around which you construct a sense of identity, you realize that your search for answers is, in itself, part of your faith pilgrimage. When you look at the amazing dimensions of Jesus' identity formation, you can take courage that He was formed in healthy ways, and that your own questioning, searching, and constructing are on target, when you go with the right issues. In this search, it is vitally important that you find safe and wholesome people to assist you in the adventure that leads to a healthy identity.

# WHO?

What am I that You think of me, a child of earth, and that You come near to me? For You made me a little lower than Your angels, and You crowned me with glory and honor. You created me and gave me dominion over the works of Your hands. . . . O Lord! How majestic is Your name in all the earth!

Psalm 8:3-9, paraphrased

---

## WHERE?

Recall the identity of your childhood years, and the question of your adolescent years, "Who am I?" Never to have asked is to forever remain locked into one's culturally defined destiny.

To your timeline, add the major identity questions in the years where they surfaced.

## WHAT?

Name two people who are important to you. Plan a storytelling time with them, to hear their journey of identity search.

## WHY?

As you have seen yourself in a developmental perspective, can you celebrate your conception and see God at work in forming you in your mother's womb, as the Psalmist did in Psalm 139?

## WHEN?

Can you find someone who will listen to your story—friend or spouse—who will support you with your uncertainties?

---

# FOUR

## SEARCHING FOR INTIMACY

Chad had signed up on the conference sheet outside my guest office door at the school where I was a three-day campus lecturer. When he came in, I was startled at how young he looked—sixteen perhaps.

"What did you want to talk about?" I asked, ready to hold back my question about his obvious youth.

"Well, your message in convocation this morning was very interesting, and someday I hope to be able to establish a relationship that leads to marriage. But right now I just need a friend. Not a girlfriend, a guy friend."

"And you don't have guy friends?"

"In a way I do, like everybody else; but I really want a friend who knows everything about me and who lets me know who he really is. Most friendships here on campus are pretty 'surfacy.' "

"Is there somebody in particular you want for such a friendship?"

"Yes, but he has a girlfriend, and even though he is my kind of guy, he doesn't have time for me every day, and I feel jealous or something. I want him to keep up his dating, but it makes me feel like a little boy when I'm left out."

"Tell me about junior high school. Where were you?" Chad expressed feelings typical to boys during the onset of pubescence—the need of a best friend of the same sex to affirm, to listen, to assure that life is coming along right.

"Our family was doing mission deputation when I was in eighth and ninth grades, so we moved a lot. I was in five different schools during junior high."

"How old are you now?"

"Just turned sixteen."

"How in the world did you get into college so young? Are you a child prodigy?"

"I started school a little young. When we finally settled in Atlanta, I was ready for tenth grade. After two weeks in the school, my parents and I agreed that it was a dangerous place—knives, guns, and violence in the hallways. So I did all of my high school courses in a little over a year using Accelerated Christian Education curriculum—at home, alone. When my folks traveled, I went with them. They were working for a world missions organization."

I looked at this healthy young man whose high mobility during early pubescense, and almost absolute isolation during the next two years, had left him empty and hungry for friendship.

"Chad, let me tell you what may have happened," I began. "You have very healthy feelings, but they have been held over from your junior high years when your family traveled and you were alone too much of the time. I think you are frightening the young man you want to be friends with. He may suspect that you are coming on to him for an intimate sexual friendship. If you could identify two or three fellows who are not yet dating and whose faces tell you that they are lonely too, you could likely build a small group. There are a lot of guys who need friendship. You aren't the only one on this campus who is ready for serious conversation and eager for something more than surface talk. And when you have established this base of friendship support, in God's time I'm sure you will be ready to reach out and establish a solid relationship with a good woman."

## CREATING COMMUNITY

It is easy to read of the Creation in Genesis and to imagine that the splitting of Adam into male and female was primarily for sexual and reproductive reasons. But the text makes it transparently clear that intimacy along with mutuality is the universal cry, not the urge to reproduce.

> "It is not good that the human should be alone. I will make for Adam a companion ‚corresponding to it." So God built up from the *pleura*. . . .
>
> And the man said, "This is now bone of my bone, flesh of my flesh. This shall be called *Isshah*, for from *Ish* was taken this."     Genesis 2:18, 23

Community was the primary motivation for dividing Adam to form the first human family. *Pleura* is the Greek word used in the Septuagint version of the Creation account for Adam's side, and also in the Gospels' descriptions of the Roman soldier opening the side of Jesus. Both the original woman and the Bride of Christ are formed as the *pleura* of the two Adams are opened. And both create community. God is pictured as the communal God: "Let us make the human in our image." And the ultimate picture God has of the human species is communal: "Let them have dominion. . . ."

God's authoritative statement appears to be grounded in the experience of the eternal Deity. "Let us . . ." tells us something about the community of the Trinity. Chad's yearning for someone who really understood him was the cry of an honest young man. We all long for such human "mirror image" friendships. While it often feels selfish, even neurotically so, each of us also yearns to be the mirror for others.

Watch children of any age seek out and approach potential friends chosen because they most nearly mirror the child's own world, similar age, and interests. Indeed, children are such magnets for friendship that they early develop what turn out to be lifelong social skills. Left in a world of adults only, a child will tend throughout life to be oriented toward relating to seniors. Given an early environment of young children, a child later will be gifted in care-giving and in establishing friendships with people a generation younger than themselves.

We all feel an urgent need for intimate friendship, and we find that our language is inadequate to describe the meanings of true friendship.

We tolerate peer love in our children, since their social demands are so persistent. But we have rarely appreciated the magic of socialization written into the human personality for the simple price of a few overnights, slumber parties, pizza bashes, and church youth group adventures. Girls may speak of their girlfriends, but social taboos do not even permit a boy to have boyfriends. Our friendship language has been so forfeited into the sexual arena that today a twenty-year-old male college sophomore who has a girlfriend is assumed to be sleeping with her. There is something radically wrong in a culture which closes off an important life experience by denying it any language for expression. '

## SEARCH FOR THE OTHER

On a calendar which is almost infallible, humans turn to search for genital intimacy around the turn of the decade as they move from teens to twenties. Erik Erikson⁴ is likely the inventor of the phrase *identity crisis* in speaking of the emerging young adult's need to break away from his absorption into parental identity and to establish a distinct identity for himself. Erickson believes that closely linked to the identity search is the search for intimacy, which is motivated by sexual yearning.

So the Creation narrative does, indeed, pull us toward the almost universal reality that it is not good for a man or a woman to be alone. However, the mirror image needs to be the other, the *hetero* opposite the self. For this cause, then, a man or woman leaves parents and is joined to the spouse. This genitally united "one flesh" is easily regarded as the microcosm of community God intends. Marriage is the cultural convention that protects "what God joins together."⁵ But the magical bond between the man and woman is the universal mystery by which God intends always to remind us that we are created for relationship and to live in community. Monogamous marriage of a male and a female establishes the ideal microcosm which images the best estate for humanity, and also mirrors mysteries about the character of God.

But some of us are alone. Not only are we unmarried, but we live alone. And worse than living alone, there are no phone calls, no one to share our high events or our tears. We burst into laughter at a thought or at an image on television, and the room rings with our solitude. We blush realizing that laughter is a human signal which is distinctly social—it necessarily requires reciprocity and partnership. We neglect our own nutrition, since eating is primarily a social, not a nutritional, event.

When Erik Erikson described intimacy, he posed a polar opposite, isolation. This means that the single person is confronted with an obligation of unusual importance and difficulty. The single person who would be fully human must find a means of achieving intimacy with integrity. It will necessarily be nongenital, but it must fulfill the need to be present to others and to receive their presence at a level of substantial and confidential support.

North American culture is decimated today with an aberration unknown in earlier cultures or in second or third world cultures today. It is the phenomenon of singles who have marched into their adult years dedicated to surviving alone while establishing genital contact with a series of partners, unless or until they choose to cash in on actual reproduction and parenthood. Any casual examination of their way of life reveals that they are avoiding intimacy like the plague. Intimacy requires absolute respect, confidentiality, instrumental commitment to support, and readiness to take the risks of supporting others regardless of their condition, their behavior, or their needs. Today's singles' culture in America is characterized by tentativeness, conditional attachment, instrumental use of each other, and "no strings attached." They go through the motions of sexual intimacy, but it is hollow and transient.

Erik Erikson described adult singles well as isolated. They are haunted by their lack of security, their loss of self-esteem, their feelings of being vulnerable and at risk, of inferiority, of shame, of fearing that they might be missing and no one would notice. While they give off signals of autonomy, even arrogant pride in their singleness, they are promiscuous, hollow people who are artfully masking their emptiness with the latest fashions. They affect a slightly exaggerated femininity or masculinity, and they carefully avoid any environment that might melt their thin protective armor which is also their masked face presented to deceive the world.

Isolated adults who fly under the banner of "singles" slip easily and often into the swinging promiscuous destruction I described above, as people who are frightened into isolation go through the physical gestures of intimacy, and remain ever more hollow, empty, and hopeless. The only integrity route for the unmarried person is to voluntarily surrender genital goals to God and offer sexual energy in the service of Jesus and His dominion. [6]

In ancient Jewish culture, singleness was abhorred and regarded as antithetical to faith. The way of responsibility led to marriage and parenthood. Religious fidelity was closely tied to marriage and family participation within the traditional ways and roles. But Jesus introduced celibacy as an honorable, if rare, "gift to the kingdom of God."

Christian celibates, unlike singles in general in our culture, are not "on the make" romantically or sexually. In Roman Catholic tradition a special role has been assigned to celibate women in holy orders: "married to the Lord," and in some orders a simple wedding ring has been worn to show that the woman is "taken." Male celibates in the priesthood have not been identified in the same way, but take a vow to imitate the model of Jesus who was celibate and spoke the Matthew 19 words from the authority of experience.

Christian celibacy is very likely a necessary covenant for the Christian single in a promiscuous age. "Laying down my sexual aspirations in behalf of the kingdom of God" would mean in our time simply determining to send every signal that yearnings for sexual intimacy and marriage themselves had been surrendered, lest they become a consuming idolatry. Either we call upon our young to make such a covenant, or we will feed them to the wild animals of a sexually deformed culture.

Premarital innocence based on a lack of success or opportunity to establish sexual contact before marriage likely does not qualify as the badge of Christian virtue. Premarital chastity may have served as a noble dream in an era which was willing to sacrifice personal responsibility on an altar of enormous individual pride. But if premarital chastity is motivated only for egocentric pride, it is not yet obedience to Jesus. Premarital abstinence out of tough self-discipline, determined to maintain technical virginity, is admirable, and at some level we can congratulate the winners who "make it to the church on time." But technical virginity is also at times the proud insignia worn by sexually addictive violators of genital intimacy.

All these options leave Christian celibacy standing alone

as an intentional celebration of sexuality through consecrating its energy to the service of God. As such, it is a highly viable strategy offering freedom to move with integrity in all human relationships. "For now, I am content to be who I am and in the marital state I find myself," is a remarkably liberating statement. People anxious about singleness are enormously vulnerable to move into sexual exploitation or to send signals which make them the targets of such exploitive misadventures.

## COMMUNITY IN THE CHURCH

But loneliness is visible not only in singles' bars and singles' ministries in the churches where isolation masks itself and pretends—going through the motions of intimacy without the gift of trust and commitment. It is also found in the crowded highrises and in superchurches everywhere. Wherever people cluster in massive crowds, anonymity thrives.

All of us celebrate the rising standards of living which are represented by the new housing in condominiums and lovely cubed city dwellings. One would logically think that when people live in a block with five hundred other families instead of five, there would be more social contact, more friendship, more healthy networks generated. But if you have lived in such a place, you know that just the opposite occurs. It is not uncommon for people who have lived three years in a condominium to know the names of no other people in their building. They may ride the same elevators, park in parallel garages, and meet in doorways as they come and go. But they have withdrawn into an almost necessary isolation to protect their identity from the crush and press of the crowds.

We are not created for crowded living, and evidently are marginally territorial. Like experimental laboratory deer mice, the more crowded our living environments get, the more we pile up and quiver in basic struggles of disorientation in our huddled living arenas. Some studies have suggested that fertility and sexual orientation may be among the first sensitive human capacities to be negatively affected by overcrowding.

When you look around you at church, see whether you can name twenty people of importance to you. Ask yourself whether you would be missed if you were wiped out in an accident on the way to church. Would they be able to put your name and face together? The trend toward congregations of thousands for a single hour of worship on Sunday morning is one we celebrate at one level. But we need to ask whether this is, indeed, the church.

If such a mass meeting satisfies a need for worshiping God, then watching a service on television in the privacy of one's own home would likely do just as well. The enormous success of the electronic church may speak both of the religious hunger of the age and of the trembling isolation of its citizens. We must ask whether intimacy needs can be met more effectively than we are presently doing.

The anonymity of the gigantic superchurch may also describe a smaller congregation that is equally indifferent to people's needs for genuine unconditional support and affirmation. So the nagging question remains: How can we take steps toward guaranteeing that the community of faith will indeed function as a community?

† We must come to terms with the need for being people of covenants. Privacy and individualism have become a way of death for North Americans.

† We must find ways of calling all people to participate in network communities of support, confidentiality, and unconditional affirmation, discipline, and nurture.

† We must make it legitimate to tell the truth, to reveal pain and failure in the network community.

† We must develop skills for generating stories from the participants, for identifying growth agendas and for processing

accountability among the participants.

Dr. James Fowler, director of the Center for the Study of Faith Development at Emory University, asserts that if a church does not provide the matrix in which clusters of unconditionally affirming groups are forming, there really is no church at all![3]

## COMMUNITY IN FAMILY

Intimacy begins at home. Unless there are serious flaws in the family, we arrive on this planet loved unconditionally. Indeed, the concept of *agape* love, the uniquely unilateral commitment to hold in positive regard, is tutored in the conception, birthing, and care-giving of the infant. We rarely contemplate how helpless and how much of a liability we were at the moment of our arrival. Yet through the mystery of parenting, we were enveloped by love, cared for before we had any consciousness of our own existence. The early years are full of profound curricula of intimacy: touch, embrace, kiss, stroking, totally encompassing and engrossing affection. The psalmist utters a primal praise for God's goodness: "He has set the solitary in families!"

In our privatistic society with its focus on nuclear families, it is easy to imagine that the placing of the solitary was in the arms of father-mother-brother-sister, the core members of what we have called a nuclear family. But in a Hebraic sense, the picture is vastly larger. To be placed in a family is to be put into a lineage that connects to the past, into an inheritance for the present, and into a linkage to the future. In all of our searching for factors which contribute to a sense of identity, there are few which are more significant than these depth connections within the family. Let me walk you through the simplest exploration of these family dimensions.

✝   Connected to the past. I walked tonight along the

Charles River in Boston. My first American forebear once grazed his sheep on Boston Commons, and Joy Street extends from the Commons out into the city. I preach tomorrow morning at Park Street Church only a few hundred yards from Joy Street. I never knew that first Boston Joy, but his seed was scattered across America and my grandfather, Charles Wesley Joy, homesteaded in Gray County, Kansas. I was delivered, the firstborn and the first grandchild, in the Joy home on that original farm southwest of Ensign.

My grandma was a Hulet, the daughter of a frontier Free Methodist evangelist and church planter. Like many preachers' daughters whose fathers are away more than they are home, she took up with a young man who didn't have strong Christian values—at least not rigorous ones like Grandma Carrie Hulet Joy's beliefs. But she pitched seven children into the world, and when the older boys were approaching their teens, she singlehandedly planted a Sunday School in the Cave school-house and arranged for some Kentucky Methodist evangelists to come for revival meetings. Grandpa was converted and together they founded the Cave Community Free Methodist Church.

I am a combination of all of that history. When I look in the mirror, at age fifty-nine, I literally see my Grandpa Joy as I knew him best, though I am less buoyant and lighthearted than he was. My Royer introversion may have endowed me with an important window into the inner world. And I am Grandma Joy's evangelist and ambassador for Jesus. She would be amazed to see that I am based in Kentucky at the very spot from which she imported those evangelists! You can see that I am rooted in name, in geography, in ethnic and faith traditions, and in ge-netic endowment that goes far beyond the nuclear Joy-Royer family in which I was given primary nurture.

† Inheritance in the present. Besides the daily reminder that I have the face and body build of Grandpa Joy and the personality of my mother's family, there are other gifts. I am a

son of the Kansas soil, of the Great Depression, and of the English-German-American tough work ethic. No financial wealth has come to me through my family, but a deeper endowment has been well transferred—the understanding that the family stands as guarantor, trustee, and collateral for me. I married at nineteen without nest egg or income. I had health, imagination, and promise of a campus franchise at the college where I would be a senior. That was enough. My tribal collateral would be my insurance and my bail money; and while I was fully adult and fully free, I knew I was not alone in the world. This view of family as resource is somewhere deep inside me at an instinctual level, and we have been glad to release our sons in much the same way. God has indeed placed me in a family as a support network, a value base, and a launching pad.

† Linkage to the future. Now I look into the faces of six grandchildren. If the times continue to be good to me, perhaps I will see their children. When I lift Justin into the air to get my arrival hug and kiss, I look into a face that I received from my Grandpa Joy. The genes have done an amazing thing—they have leapfrogged twice in a hundred years. And who knows how many times more they leaped in centuries before that. I can trace the genetic characteristics of Heather, Lesli, Jason, Jami, and Jordan and can celebrate their linkup with history. Jami has my mother's face and my father's contagious personality. Lesli is a beautiful combination of her mother's lighthearted loveliness and her Grandma Robbie's looks and extraversion. We watch them moving into their own futures, knowing that we are going with them. It is stunning to consider that whatever gifts of ours were needed in the world will still be there to serve in new skin but with merely transformed faces and ways. It is hard to feel old or alone when I contemplate how graciously I have been set in a "family."

I have given these vignettes, not because they are unique or wonderful, but for the opposite reason. All of us have

been placed in a family. Your connections may be more celebrated than my own. But occasionally someone is an orphan; if
not literally, they may be orphaned emotionally. And the wonderful thing about being human is that we are able to pick up
connectedness with replacement families. Here are three
examples.

† "I was very thankful for Sharon's family," Mark told me.
"My family was so disturbed and troubled that I really felt the
need of a family. When I found Sharon, I fell in love with her,
but I was ecstatic to meet a family that immediately adopted me
in. For twenty years I have finally felt human because I have a
functioning family."

† "What can I call you?" It was a question from the nine-
teen-year-old daughter of Al's second wife. She was asking the
father of her new daddy, who had officiated at the private
wedding. "I knew she had no living grandparents, so I said,
'Would you like to call me Grandpa?' " Lyle reported that she
immediately embraced him, sobbing lightly, and whispered
"Grandpa" repeatedly into his ear.

† "We have no relatives within a thousand miles of here,"
Sandra commented over dinner in their home, "but we have
adopted surrogate parents to link up with our kids. The Joneses
have grandchildren of their own in Minnesota and they see
them only a few days out of the year. Our kids see them three
times a week and love them. The kids drag them to the car after
church on Sunday mornings, insisting that we drive them
home."

## HEALING IN COMMUNITY

We all need a community of intimacy. Try as we may to insulate ourselves from other people and to display an iron-man
approach to autonomy and individualism, we always fail. We
need people. We need supportive network communities. And

we are at peace only when we sense the connections that family relatedness provides for us.

When things go wrong, when stress or anxiety burn through our energy and immobilize us, we may turn to private therapy for healing. But in most cases, healing tends to happen more quickly and at a deeper level in community. Therapists today are more alert than ever before to suggest group sessions, in which they build community through shared stories and mutual covenants of support. The addiction support groups spawned out of the "Twelve-Step Anonymous" programs of Alcoholics Anonymous all work on a network support group base. Today there are anonymous groups not only for alcoholics, but for homosexuals, people suffering from food disorders, sexual addicts, and people in hundreds of other problem situations.

Self-help groups are not new. Two hundred years ago John Wesley had established class meetings and specialized cell groups of alcoholics and other personal and social disorders. Virtually all of the early Methodist leaders and pastors came through these network support and accountability groups.

Today, let us celebrate our intimacy connections and our grounding in significant covenant groups. When Jesus wanted to change the course of history on this planet, He chose to work with a dozen people in an intimate network. There is scarcely any suggestion that He involved them in anything that resembled schooling, formal instruction, or our idea of spiritual disciplines. Instead, they were committed to each other, came to know each other profoundly well, and were affirmed into eternal memory when Jesus no longer called them servants, but friends.

# WHO?

There was a person all alone, having neither child nor sibling. There was no end to the toil, yet the accumulating wealth was not satisfying, "For whom am I working," the person said, "and why am I depriving myself of meaningful relationship?   Ecclesiastes 3:8-12, paraphrased

## WHERE?

On a piece of paper, label the four sides, Family—first degree; Lifelong friends; family—second and third degree; Work, Club, Church. Under each heading list at least five names of people you are in contact with often. First-degree relatives are spouse, parent, child, sibling.

## WHAT?

You just drew a picture of your hand-held trampoline. These are the people who hold your support network—rejoicing with you over peak experiences and weeping with you when pain or trouble hits. Are you sufficiently in touch with them?

## WHY?

Reflect now on a time when you were most discouraged, even depressed. Who walked with you through the valley of the shadow of that pain? "God has placed the solitary in families."

## WHEN?

Whose trampolines are you holding?

# FIVE

## AVOIDING THE PLEASURE TRAP

During my eighteen years at Asbury Theological Seminary, I have taught more than a thousand people who became pastors, several hundred ministers of education, more than a dozen college and seminary professors, and six college deans. But there have been others. And a handful of the dropouts still haunt my memory.

Gary never took a class with me, but he tracked me down following an amazing one-hour session in which he thought a senior professor attacked me. Gary followed me from that professor's classroom where I had been a guest. At three that afternoon, he returned to my office and was still there at six-thirty. During these hours the conversation turned so that I, the one rescued by his compassion, began to hear Gary's story of pain and vulnerability.

I learned, for example, that he was a preacher's kid from a very impressive pastoral lineage. He had lived at home while attending college, so that when he came to seminary at twenty-three, it was his first time out of the house. He jumped at the offer made on campus by a representative of a book company, and found himself the national grand champion salesman at the end of the summer. He made a bundle of money, and started his second year driving a shiny Thunderbird. He also hit the fast lane. I found out later that when we parted, he headed for a singles' bar in Lexington—a recently acquired pattern. So within a week of our first meeting, I was carrying the load of watching him slip beneath the wheel of his appetites, hearing of his serial alliances with women he met in the bars, and his disenchantment with seminary and his vision of ministry.

His second year went unfinished, as courses turned into incompletes and eventually into academic failures. At the last minute, he hit my house to ask whether he could leave a half dozen boxes and a few hanging clothes in a closet. He was off to make his second bundle of money with the summer book sales.

But Gary walked off his sales district in August without making the final round to deliver the books and to close his financial records for the company and the clients. He disappeared from my world for a few months, until I learned he was in California. Ken, a lifelong friend of Gary who knew the details of his recent choices at least as well as I did, stopped by with an address. I suggested we sit down and on the spot write to Gary and then pray for him.

There was no response to the letters, and it was perhaps three or four years before I heard Gary's voice on the phone. "I'm in Lexington. Could I drive out and pick up my things I left with you?"

"Of course, and come for supper and spend the night with us."

He declined the hospitality. He was in a hurry, he said, but as the two of us stood by his car in the driveway as he was leaving, he blurted out the truth. "I've never deceived you about anything before, and I'm not going to start now," he said. "I'm traveling with a woman, and she's waiting for me at a motel in Lexington. I'm sorry, but I can't stay."

Gary had made choices that had consequences, and these consequences limited his present options. It was simply too painful for him to turn around and face the dominoes falling on him.

Today I am still putting together what I know about Gary. He traveled for a time with a wealthy woman almost three times his age. Then there was a live-in with off-and-on-again separations. Finally, another, before repentance, conversion, marriage, and his wife's amazing plunge into Christian faith.

I sat recently in their home, two young children in my lap, a third on the way. Gary and his wife are lay directors of the youth department at their church. Gary has thickened and aged, but his face is clear and he is at peace. Life is good and grace is everywhere. In some ways I have trouble with memories and with wondering what might have been. But he looks like a man truly brought back from the dead, so it is easy to rejoice and celebrate God's grace.

## FREE TO CHOOSE

When it comes to choices, we tend to see options in polarity—right and wrong, black and white, good and evil. It was their great leader Moses who told the Children of Israel, "I have set before you life and death, blessings and curses" (Deuteronomy 30:19).

In *The Great Divorce*, C.S. Lewis wrote of a busload of people who visited hell. One by one the citizens of hell told why they were unable to forget or forgive, why they persisted in being right, or why they wrote theological papers even in hell. As the tour guide explained the amazing resistance of the hellbent people, he said, "There are only two kinds of people in the end: those who say to God, 'Thy will be done,' and those to whom God says, in the end, 'Thy will be done.' "[1]

Those were Gary's options, and he finally threw in the towel on having it his way and cried out, "Your will be done!" When I think of Gary I sometimes think also of an amazing narrative of warning in Hebrews 12:14-17, here paraphrased.

Make every effort to live in peace with everyone and to be holy; for without holiness no one will see the Lord. See to it that no one misses the grace of God and that no wild seed grows up to cause trouble and defile many. See that no one is a fornicator, or is worldly minded like Esau, who for a single meal sold his inheritance rights as the oldest son. Afterward, as you know, when he wanted to inherit this blessing, he was rejected. He found no place of repentance, though he sought the blessing with tears.

All of us have an appetite for freedom. Indeed, the American way of life celebrates freedom. And in its present form, freedom is often regarded as a right with few responsibilities. But choices necessarily have consequences, and all of us know that at some level there is no free lunch, that eventually we must step forward and pay. *I can choose the fast lane, but I cannot choose the consequences!*

"You have at least two options that I can see," I said to Bill, torn between his wife and a woman he had seduced.

"But I can't seem to decide which way to go. I just hope that tomorrow will take care of everything."

I went to some trouble to sort out the complicated issues, and then said, "I suggest you make a decision about your marriage, and then make another separate decision about the other relationship." But he seemed able to operate only by daily drift. Even the decision not to decide was a decision with consequences—in his case moving from one degree of chaos and pain to monumentally greater tragedy and chaos.

We had a neighbor once who, after twenty years of punching a time clock in the city, moved to an adjoining farm. He was appalled to find that his fields came up with a solid cover of weeds in the spring. "Who planted these weeds?" he asked my father. Dad laughed. "You don't have to plant weeds," he responded. "They are always there."

In the Esau illustration from the Book of Hebrews, the caution about choices runs especially toward a warning about indifference, about not choosing, yet choosing. "See that no one misses the grace of God and that no wild weed grows up to cause trouble and defile many."

Here is a passive road to hell, without hint of rebellion or bad spirit. Edmund Burke's words, "All that is necessary for the forces of evil to win in the world is for enough good men to do nothing!" warn of the central tendency toward destruction in corporate settings—the nation, the community, the church, and the family. But it is true also at the personal level. Daniel T. Niles' book on the nature and work of evil, *On Leaving It to the Snake*, stresses that sin, and especially what we call the original sin, is often passive. That is, it forfeits making a choice in favor of a no-decision strategy. And forfeiture is a double tragedy because it misses the grace of God, and produces a harvest of weeds.

## *THE PULL OF* NEPHESH

There is an amazing and largely underdeveloped image in the Creation narrative. God breathes into Adam "the breath of life" and Adam becomes a "living soul" or *nephesh*, or a "thing alive." But when the search is on for a companion "corresponding to Adam," it leads to an examination of the animal kingdom, also created on the sixth day. As he looks over the animals, Adam gives a name to "every living *nephesh*." Animal life and human life have a profound common characteristic—*nephesh*. To be a "thing alive" is to be aware of the driving demands of being a warm-blooded, appetite-driven mammal. When humans are described as having primal needs or drives, the descriptions are animal or *nephesh* descriptions. But what is distinctive about humans is that they have the capacity to assert will and value choices over physiological needs and appetites, though many of us behave at times in sheerly *nephesh* ways.

However much any of us is frightened by the debate about human connection to animals, we are solidly locked into the sixth day in which the *nephesh* creation was formed—both animal and human.

One of the painful realities any of us must face is this: *My appetites for instant pleasure are sure to blow up my future.*

There is a striking use of *nephesh* in Genesis 14. Abraham had voluntarily and as an act of thanksgiving paid a tithe to Melchizedek, King of Salem. The King of Salem ruled what we know as Jerusalem, and we celebrate the honor that Melchizedek gets when he is lifted up as an early model on the order of Jesus (Hebrews 5:6).

Abraham was then approached by the King of Sodom, ruler of the sexually corrupted culture of the ancient world. He obviously had heard of Abraham's generous and voluntary tax tithe paid to Melchizedek. But the King of Sodom was after something else. "Give me the *nephesh* of every person, and keep the goods for yourself" (Genesis 14:21). A tithe is indeed a modest gift to make compared to running the risk of being pulled into the whirling vortex of the downward spiral of sensuous pleasure—the clear objective of the King of Sodom. The King of Sodom wanted their spirits, to seduce them into animal reflex appetites. And what we know about addictive seduction, whether it is for sex, food, the lottery or other gambling, is that when the King of Sodom gets our *nephesh*, he gets everything else, including our money.

Dag Hammarskjold has left us an amazing legacy in his *Markings*. But the crown jewel of that reflective collection of his writings is to the point of the *nephesh* appetite.

> You cannot play with the animal in you
> without becoming wholly animal,

play with falsehood
without forfeiting your right to truth,

play with cruelty
without losing your sensitivity of mind.

He who wants to keep his garden tidy
doesn't reserve a plot for weeds. [2]

Esau's appetites, as portrayed in Genesis 25, seem understandable, even normal. A hungry man strikes a deal with his brother in exchange for a bowl of beans. His physical appetite seems harmless enough. But the writer of the Book of Hebrews puts the camera on Esau to illustrate the serious folly of imagining that intangible future reality can be bartered away for present and instant gratification of physical desire. This evidently makes Esau a "worldly person."

But the writer of Hebrews adds an accusation to the bill of particulars against Esau—he was a fornicator. And here we simply have to give up. We know nothing of Esau's sex life, except that he had taken up with "the daughters of Heth," and his mother was distressed at the prospect that Jacob would do the same. (See Genesis 27:46.) Our misunderstandings about fornication get in the way of our seeing the likely central issue. Fornication consistently expresses a tragedy quite different from premarital sex. It denotes instead a tendency to reduce people to objects. This reductionism has an immediate effect we call low self-esteem.

The Hebrew and Greek words translated as fornication in the King James Version consistently refer not to premarital sex, but to promiscuous, instrumental use of persons for sheer gratification of sexual pleasure. We brought the Greek word into English as "porn-ography." But in the process, the first letter was changed, in the same shift that turned *piscus* to "fish."

*Porneia* became "fornication."

In Proverbs 6:26, for example, "The fornicator reduces you to a loaf of bread" tells the story of the loss of a sense of dignity, value, and self-respect. And in an ironic twist, it is not the fornicator or prostitute who is reduced to a "loaf of bread" or a "steak dinner" or an "evening out," but the user of the fornicator. By treating another person as an object, I have reduced myself to the same value I placed on him or her.

So Esau was, by his biological impulse for instant gratification through food, reducing himself to a mere object—an appetite to be served. As such, fornicator becomes a name to describe idolatry. And fornication and idolatry are frequently linked in Scripture.

Some time ago I got a piece of mail. I get a lot of junk mail, but this one was pretty magnetic. The return address slipped past me, simply PBC with an address. But the punch line seemed to be in mile-high letters:

For the man who wants it all. Now!

On the reverse side, in full color, was a healthy looking fellow and now the words were more direct and first person:

"I want it all, and I want it now!"

Inside were books and other products calculated to make me such a man: books on management, how to dress for success, how to climb the corporate ladder, and special books on how to beat the IRS. There were other exotic titles, and they were pictured in lovely color jackets, offered as a Playboy Book Club special. I could have had my choice of any four of these for $2.98.

*The Green Ripper*
*The Day the Bubble Burst*
*Men's Bodies*
*Nothing Lasts Forever*
*Diary of a Virgin* by Cindy Peach

If the last was a pseudonym, I was surprised it wasn't

credited to Eve Apple, but that gives you some idea of the power of the *nephesh* pull. It was appealing to the Esau in me—to the fallen, Spirit-emptied animal impulses in me—competition, greed, exploitation, narcissism, and dominance.

Esau's vulnerability was that he wanted it all. Now! Maybe that is the real definition of worldly minded—to regard this present world as "all there is," and to take a tragically terminal view of reality. If we are willing to settle for a tangible, transient, sensuous experience as the ultimate reality, we will likely get it, one way or another.

We sometimes think of worldliness as a matter of being secular. I used to think that being secular meant that you weren't religious. But secular has nothing to do with being religious. To be secular means to be in pursuit of a god or a target which is moving on an unpredictable and unproven course. To be secularized is to be without a known harbor, without goal, without target, to be "lost in space."[3] The opposite of secular is cyclical or predictable, having perhaps irregular turns but coming out at a known goal at a specific calculated harbor.

We live in a culture without targets or clear goals toward which we are moving. The secular culture is often involved only in maintenance, without commitment to responsibility for future effects of present choices. But secular culture tends not to ask long-term questions about destinies, about the worthwhileness of the journey.

When Christian young people shift from a fairly cyclical, predictable value system of home and community into the new environment of the university or the city, they find it easier to yield to the Esau appetite, the secular trend, and the *nephesh* spirit. John Wesley's mother must have detected such a pull on him early in his tour as a student at Oxford University. In one of her letters she wrote to him,

Would you judge the lawfulness or unlawfulness

of any pleasure, take this rule:
Whatever weakens your reason,
impairs the tenderness of your conscience,
obscures your sense of God,
or takes off the relish of spiritual things;
in short, whatever increases the strength and
authority of your body over your mind,
that thing is sin to you,
however innocent it may be in itself.

## COMING BACK FROM NEPHESH ADDICTION

To the Ephesian Christians, St. Paul issues an ultimatum: "Do not be drunk with wine (feeding the *nephesh* appetite), but be filled with the Spirit" (accepting the alternative grace-driven motivation and an appetite for what is just, true, and holy).

The human tendency to drift into the squirrel-cage existence that comes from "serving the appetites of mere *nephesh*" is universal. We are vulnerable to becoming compulsively hooked in a thousand ways. Indeed, addiction research has revealed what we must have suspected—that the addictive personality is likely to have accumulated a cluster of parallel addictions. Eighty percent of addicts have two pathological specific addictions. Sixty percent have three. And if the person goes "on the wagon" with one of the addictions, the compulsive behavior tends to explode into one of the other addictions.

Church congregations and other communities committed to human welfare are finding that their ministry virtually requires that they develop skill in diagnosing addiction and then put together the support system which is necessary to break the addiction cycle.

Compulsive behavior is rooted in a severely damaged core of personality. It would be too simple to call it low self-

tently visible symptom. When we look at the "addiction behavior cycle," we can see where self-esteem went.

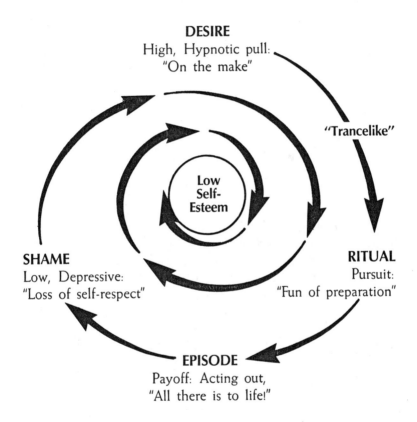

**DESIRE**
High, Hypnotic pull:
"On the make"

"Trancelike"

Low
Self-
Esteem

**SHAME**
Low, Depressive:
"Loss of self-respect"

**RITUAL**
Pursuit:
"Fun of preparation"

**EPISODE**
Payoff: Acting out,
"All there is to life!"

This cycle of the pattern of addictive behavior is adapted from the work of Patrick Carnes[4] of Golden Valley Hospital in Minneapolis/St. Paul. His pioneering work with sexual addiction has actually recovered the small group healing pattern of

tion has actually recovered the small group healing pattern of the class meeting established as part of the early Methodist movement in England. There, John Wesley clustered people by geographic areas to maintain a support for their new Christian discipleship. But he also pulled together special groups by specific lifestyle problems. There are records, for example, of classes made up of recovering alcoholics. Both Carnes' work and E. Mansell Pattison's study of ex-gays who have been transformed into heterosexual orientation, utilize the group support system so essential for healing. [5]

It should not surprise us to find that people gripped by the *nephesh* reduction to animal-like appetite addiction are rescued and restored to their true humanity in face-to-face support groups which

† listen to a complete documentation of the addictive history with its lifelong roots,

† articulate explicit forgiveness and affirm hope for a new and restored vision and actual new life, and

† declare unconditional commitment to support, to hold accountable, and to serve as emergency rescuers should the addiction take over temporarily at any point in the future.

A well-known minister phoned me to question the meanings of fornication and adultery, [6] as they applied to a prominent leader in his community. After nearly an hour of consultation, it became clear that the leader was sexually addicted. The caller said, "I know what we've got to do!"

I had virtually forgotten the call until two years later when I was lecturing at a college. Two students introduced themselves as children of the minister who had phoned. I was delighted to meet them. Then, on the way to the airport, the man who drove me reported the rest of the story, although he did not know of my consultation nearly two years before. "The pastor phoned me," he said, "and called four of us together. We sat dumbfounded as he outlined a strategy. We went to the resort hotel where our mutual friend had holed up with the latest woman in his sexual adventures. His wife was distraught, of course, having gone through this repeatedly across the years. We phoned his room and identified ourselves and told him we were there to take him home. We would not take no for an answer, and were going to see him through to complete integrity. Well, last Wednesday night after church, this fellow grabbed my wife and me. He put his head on my shoulder and cried, and thanked me for bringing him home and sticking with him. We meet with him a couple of times a month just to keep the honesty up-to-date. It has been a tremendous battle for him, but the power of that addiction is finally letting go."

## *LOST ORIENTATION*

There seems to be an irreversible fatalism in the Hebrews text suggesting that Esau was at a point of no return. The ultimate tragedy of life is that *if I lose sight of my goals, I may never find the way home!* The commentary in Hebrews is graphic and painful: "Afterward, as you know, when Esau wanted to inherit this blessing, he was rejected." Esau was so disoriented that he was unable to take initiatives headed toward home. "He found no place of repentance, though he sought the blessing diligently and with tears." On this side of the Cross and Resurrection, we can at least say that no one finds their way home alone. It is in community that we get our bearings, and it is in community that we discover that we do, indeed, have value. [7]

Imagine how different the outcome, if the text could have reported, "Esau accepted the reality of the lost blessing, but he found a place of repentance and returned to the dignity of his vocation from that time on." The critical key may have been his inability to find his way home. If so, the real tragedy of pursuing the *nephesh* path is the disorientation of forgetting what is true, good, honest, and of value. Disoriented people tend to be preoccupied with status, recouping losses, and holding on to old grudges. And when those past failures and problems become a mania, they cannot see the place of repentance and so cannot get back on the track of a life that will have meaning from this point on.

A few years ago, I was pained at the news story of a light plane which left Shreveport bound for New Orleans with the pilot and one passenger on board. When the flight was several hours overdue, an alert was signaled through the air traffic control network. A commercial pilot reported having noted the plane's identification as it was heading out to sea over the Atlantic Ocean. It was never found. In our lives as well, we can get off course, onto paths which never lead to home or to ultimate goals worth pursuing.

## WAYS BACK TO PEACE AND HOLINESS

The pessimism of the Esau story breaks when we go back to the beginning of the teaching passage. And the formula for making sense of disorder is straightforward: *If I want to keep my perspective clear, holiness is the only way!* "Make every effort to live in peace with everyone and to be holy; for without holiness no one will see the Lord."

The King James Version speaks of "pursuing" peace and "holiness without which no man shall see the Lord." Here is the orientation or direction signal again. Life is, indeed, a pilgrimage. We are in motion. Life is the curriculum. And our choices involve direction. If God demanded that we achieve distinction as peacemakers, or that we be visibly and perfectly holy, we would choke and stumble. But the call is to "make every effort." It would be comforting if we could count on some sort of celestial transaction to take care of our peace and holiness in heaven's computer terminal. But while grace originates with God and works in two worlds, it is clear that the call also demands a human response, even an initiative. To obey Jesus requires not simply a singular choosing, but demands choices that continue day by day.

It is urgent that we link our vision and our choices to God's calling to integrity, holiness, and peacemaking. As people with a high need for celebration, happiness, and pleasure, it is painful for us to admit that we also have a capacity for becoming compulsive about unnatural "highs" and falling into addiction to the animal within. But Jesus has given us a better Spirit than false spirits which addict us to destructive ways of living and relating to each other. By grace, and with the support of our networks of accountability and affirmation, we can avoid the pleasure trap.

# Who?

Be not drunk with wine, food, sex, or debilitating substances, but be filled with the Spirit of God!                    Ephesians 5:18, paraphrased

---

## WHERE?

Turn back to the timeline you began in chapter 1. On it plot symbols at ages when you felt very vulnerable to slipping into the pleasure trap. Review the decisions you made at each point. Where was God's grace in each case?

## WHAT?

Are you fulfilling the Creation mandate to "have dominion" or to "take charge here" by affirming and stabilizing some of the teenagers you know?

## WHY?

How do you account for the human tendency to laziness and the path of least resistance, and for the ease with which we nurture the *nephesh* or animal spirit in ourselves?

## WHEN?

Jesus warned that anyone who caused a little one to stumble would be better off thrown into the ocean with a mill stone tied around the neck. What can you do to defuse the pleasure traps laid for your young friends?

---

# S I X

## ENGAGING THE VOCATION

The Friday evening vespers at Parched Corn Overlook were winding down. On Wednesday night, Doug had confessed his confusion about how I could predict the day on which we would see our first teen backpacker openly inquire about Jesus and make a spontaneous faith commitment. Now, on Friday night, we had looped back, with a grand climactic trip to Rock Bridge, complete with a couple of hours playing in the waterfalls.

In the Holy Communion Covenant Service during vespers, it was easy for new believers to report on their faith commitments made late in the week. They were sitting by trail families of eight, five teens and three of my students who comprised the week-long work and accountability network in which we lived. Three probationers from an Indiana county had been placed in separate trail families, and their sponsor, a county judge, in yet another network. Now each of the probationers had spoken, interspersed with a dozen others.

Finally, Judge Jonathan Palmer stood and faced to us, his background a late summer sunset. "Last spring, when I learned of your backpacking trip, I asked the three fellows with me whether they would like to come at the court's expense. When they agreed, I worried a little, hoping that they would have a good time. I hoped that I would be able simply to complete the week of hiking ten to fifteen miles each day. But I had not dreamed of going home with the deep changes the guys have reported here tonight." As we stood for a final vesper prayer, trail families spontaneously linked arms in fellowship circles, while our guitarists led off with our favorite Scripture songs learned through the week.

As we sang, I remembered conversations Jonathan and Donna Palmer had initiated with Robbie and me ten winters before, as they wrestled with a deep sense of identity and mission. Donna, a social worker, was in hand-to-hand contact with profound human needs on a daily basis in the Lexington-Fayette County Health Department. Jonathan was in seminary, headed for one of the most secure ministry jobs anyone could find—a conference appointed pastoral position in a midwestern state.

I was totally unprepared when Jonathan said, "I am thinking of leaving seminary and applying to law school."

"What is going on? What seems attractive about law school?"

"It isn't so attractive, I guess. It's just that when I see how the system works against poor and really troubled people, I think maybe Jesus wants me to get ready to put some pressure on the system. I would like to make a speciality of looking after the disenfranchised, those who almost never get decent legal help. Donna sees them every day. The system works fairly well for people who have a bank account."

Across several months Jonathan and Donna processed the vision, and the law school applications went out. After graduation from law school, Jonathan was appointed to fill the unexpired term of a judge who went out of office prematurely. He later ran as a candidate to succeed himself. His probation campers were a small but highly personalized chapter of his current life mission.

## VOCATION—WHAT IS IT?

Vocation commonly refers to a job or a calling. But among Christians we know that vocation is deeper than the idea of a job. *Vocation* is roughly the equivalent of "meaning." Each of us asks, "Why am I here?" and if we find a compelling answer, we have found our vocation, our reason for being.

It is sometimes said that being a Christian is the ultimate vocation.¹ And there simply must be a connection between deep spiritual and religious grounding and a sense of vocation. But people who grasp at religious faith as a drowning person hangs on for life, frequently experience insecurity about root issues of being, meaning, and destiny.

We sometimes use vocation to describe our deep sense of calling which transcends a present job or task. You might be a wife and mother, but embrace your vocation as a humanitarian. In doing so you would be telling us that your volunteer work with the Florence Crittenden Home is what gives you your primary sense of meaning in life, and likely that homemaking and mothering are less urgent tasks now that your youngest is off to college. My cousin, a top-notch diesel mechanic, tells me that he takes his paycheck from GM Diesel, but lives to do the work of an evangelist. By this he means teaching Bible studies with searching people he recruits in making follow-up calls for his church. His vocation is that of an evangelist.

## GROUNDING A SENSE OF IDENTITY AND MEANING

For most of human history, an infant was born into a fixed station in life. To grow up within the family was to take on its identity and find meaning by perpetuating its traditions.

In this transmission of vocation, there was little probability of failure or of frustration. Each person knew early on what life expected, and developed the necessary skills to be worthwhile and useful members of the community. Indeed, some social and religious critics sometimes deplore the diversity open to today's student generation, and long for a return to the old days when status and role were determined, and no choices were permitted. At least then we didn't need vocational counselors, psychiatrists, or self-esteem counseling.[2]

In most of the world today, children are born into vocation. If we object that this represents a terrible determinism, a devaluing of the individual, or a waste of human potential, we should also look at the benefits. Few such people suffer from identity confusion, burnout, or job dissatisfaction; and most seem to take delight in the simple pleasures of begetting children and training them to take up their tools or their trades in the future.

As citizens of the Western, English-speaking world, we are part of the minority who wrestle individually to find meaning. We celebrate the individual choice that comes with the territory. And we nurture the idea from early childhood that our own children deserve the right to formulate dreams of what they can become. This affirmation of freedom and responsibility certainly taps into the deepest wells of self-esteem and nourishes the vision that we each can make a difference. It perhaps even evokes Mordecai's advice to Esther, "You were born for such a time as this." The search for identity and meaning on an individual basis underscores our belief in the enormous value and potential of each person. It also cries aloud the truth that God creates life and has a purpose for each person who comes into the world.

That night when Joe and I sat at my kitchen table, I found myself saying to him, "It is no mistake that you were conceived and born. God gave you your considerable talents and your beautiful personality." I was quietly giving feedback to a kid who grew up scared, illegitimate by conception and birth, adopted, rejected by one man, and refused a surname by his current step-father. He was a runaway, a convicted auto thief, a Pendleton youth prison survivor, and a drug addict.

There have been times when I have wondered whether I

spoke the truth to Joe that night. He lived with us briefly and was gone again. Now and then the FBI would phone asking whether we knew his whereabouts. Occasionally Joe would call, sometimes using phones to which he had no legitimate access, we later learned. Today Joe has his own business and is in tune with his native gifts. I keep his business card in my file—Joe Maxwell and Son.

It is clear that vocation means identifying our gifts and putting them to work in our world. But vocation requires first some sense of who *we* are, as well as what our gifts are. If we see only a bundle of gifts, we take a functional, utilitarian view of ourselves; when gifts fade or a disability strikes, then our utility is weakened or lost and our sense of life and vocation evaporates. The foundation for vocation has to include *being* as well as *doing*.[3]

A sense of self or personal value is an elusive reality. If all of the books on self-esteem were laid end to end, we still would not know much about where this critical sense is formed. The clan surely transmitted a sense of being, by simply imprinting the cultural values, stories, and images which contained the core of their corporate life.

Today, questions of "what a woman does" and "what a man does" are critical issues that must be settled deep in the self and without the help of the clan. The answers have less to do with what people say about sexual identity and sex role than with what is demonstrated and imprinted by others into the young. "I am woman" is an early affirmation in the spirit of a little girl who is imprinted with consistent and pervasive images of womanhood and femininity within her culture. "I am man" is also easily learned if adult males are readily available, as they rarely are for most young boys in our culture.

So as we explore this critical search for vocation, it will be important for us to look at continuing ways of grounding ourselves and our young in their sense of identity and in affirming their search for meaning.

## *PURSUING THE DREAM*

In his famous study of more than forty men, Daniel Levinson of Yale found that at the age of twenty, all of them had a distinct life dream. Many of them reported seeing themselves as if on stage, often performing fantastic feats to express their unique- ness. As the third decade of life unfolded, each of the men worked through a modification of the dream to adjust it to the realities of opportunity and gifts and luck. [4]

Levinson's study seems to underscore the diversity of vision of which humans are capable. We could deplore such wild and fantastic dreaming in each generation, pointing out how much energy is wasted when kids wrestle with thousands of life-dream options. But there is a sense in which the Creation revisits every person at adolescence, as they listen to the pulsat- ing words from God, "Take charge! Have dominion! You are responsible!" It is important that adults protect the environments in which the dreams arise, while at the same time underscoring the deeper meaning of vocation.

A thirteen-year-old looking into the mirror and asking, "What am I going to do with what I've got?" is articulating a question about *gifts*. It is easy for this question to ignite a flash fire of pride, even arrogance. But most youngsters struggle enough with a sense of inferiority and helplessness that the question clangs a tone that asks, "How could anyone respect me? How can I ever achieve anything important? Who will pay attention to such an unattractive, misshapen person as me?"

Any discovery of worth in ourselves at thirteen or thirty-five is a discovery that personhood is a gift. If we have any value at all, it is grounded in what we have been given, not in what we have made of ourselves. This is the foundational idea of Christian vocation. "The whole process of discovering and nurturing and fulfilling our vocation in Christ is a matter of grace. Vocation is not something we can hope to create; rather, it is a gift which God empowers us both to receive and to perfect. All of life, when lived vocationally in Christ, is prayer."[5]

It is reasonable to say that every person who wrestles with the issue of living out the best dream is likely wrestling with grace and with God. If so, issues of vocation are ultimately resolved through prayer—negotiating the use of created humanity with the ultimate Creator of those gifts.

Taking this view of vocation as a gift of God that is invested with fulfillment and meaning only as God enters into the person's life, Paul Chilcote offers two more constructs. A *call* is less to a specific job or task than to obedience and discipleship. The call is a distinct summons which propels the individual into *community*.

> Those who believe are not only called out of darkness and death, but into fellowship with a crucified Lord, into a communion (*community*) of martyrs (literally witnesses) of the faith, and into a freedom that is bondage to love. Nowhere is the corporate nature of our vocation more visible than in our solidarity with the least, and the last, and the lost of the world.[6]

It is likely our Western privatism that runs vocation aground, just as it begins to respond to the dream which comes to us at puberty and again at mid-life. We take ourselves individually too seriously. In *The Different Drum*, psychiatrist M. Scott Peck, makes a compelling appeal for establishing community.

> Start communities. . . . Don't worry for the moment about what to do beyond that. Don't worry about

which peace group to join. Don't worry about
whether to withhold taxes, blockade a missile plant,
march in a demonstration, or write a letter to your
congressman. Don't worry much yet about feeding
the poor, housing the homeless, protecting the
abused. It is not that such actions are wrong or even
unnecessary. It is simply that they are not primary.
They are not likely to succeed unless they are
grounded, one way or another, in community. Form
a community first . . . don't feel you have to do anything. Remember that being takes precedence over
doing.[7]

Because we are created for community, the ultimate human vocation is to find significance in relationship. The Christian vision is uniquely grounded in this Creation-based, Re-
demption-forged conception—to see ourselves as intimate ex-
tensions of God's creative energy in our corner of the universe,
and to see reconciliation with God as having been made in
Jesus.

In his widely acclaimed faith development theory, James
W. Fowler says that mature adult Christian faith sees vocation
as partnership. He regards the "destiny" and "self-actualization"
visions of human purpose as

our most serious heresy, the individualistic assumption that we are or can be self-grounded persons.
This assumption means believing that we have within
us—and are totally responsible for generating from
within us—all the resources of which to create a
fulfilled and self-actualized life. It is in contrast to
this enticing, but finally illusory, strategy that I want
to . . . suggest that vocation, seen as a call to partnership with God on behalf of the neighbor, consti-

tutes a far more fruitful way to look at the question
of our specialness, and our giftedness, and our possibilities of excellence.[8]

What emerges in this foundational look at vocation is a
clear sense that there is no such thing as lone ranger spiritual
formation, and that as we walk on, we must be careful not to
walk alone. Privatism in spiritual disciplines may, eventually,
pull us away from community. Far from validating privatism
even in prayer, Jesus preferred to be joined in a community of
prayer, and was devastated on one recorded occasion to find
that His support network had abandoned Him and had fallen
asleep.

There are risks, to be sure, of parading piety in front of
groups; but pharisaism in public is in no sense even close to
community. Fowler's descriptions of the person who accepts
vocation as "partnership" with God will make the issue clearer. If
we undertake living with a sense of "vocation," our lives will be
characterized by:

† Sensing that we are called to excellence that has no
grounding in competition with other people. Our vocation is
distinct from others' vocations, not by comparison of accomplishment, but by assessing God's gifts and energy given to us
and then being faithful to those gifts.

† Not worrying that someone else will beat us to the top
in setting records or making a name. Given the enormous field
of tasks which need urgently to be done, there is no need to be
jealous about who gets there first or who receives credit. We
can unconditionally rejoice with those who achieve.

† Rejoicing in the gifts and graces of others, knowing that
their gifts and graces are for the good of the whole community.
We are, as Fowler terms it, all involved in an "ecology of giftedness" for the common good.

† Celebrating the gifts of others, for we are freed from

the neurotic sense that we have to be "multigifted" and "do what everybody expects us to do." In the community we know that the gifts of others are available, so none of us needs to do everything.

† Seeing our gifts within the context of community and knowing that we are liberated to "seek a responsible balance" in the ways we use our time and energy. None of us has to "save the whole world!" The Christian vocation is realistic, whereas workaholism is a sure sign of a lost vision. When Mother Theresa was told that the children she was caring for would die eventually because of lack of funds to care for them, she said, I am not ultimately responsible for what happens to the children. But I am responsible for what happens to them today while they are in my care. So I will feed them and caress them today."

† Regarding time as a gift and thus being freed from the tyranny of time. To be settled into the vocation of partnership with God and others is to sense that the duration of life, even, is a matter of gift and of stewardship. So, instead of a frantic approach to mid-life, or to a career change, or to retooling in more schooling, the luxury of faithfulness today is enough. We are not responsible for getting done everything that we can see. We are responsible for taking steps appropriate within the time we have, given the vision of our gifts that the community and God help us to see.

† Changing careers, if necessary, to fit a pattern of growth and vision about our gifts and responsibilities that is consistent with the Christian vocation. We can regard it as healthy that we discover at thirty gifts we were quite unaware of at thirteen. "Our life structures," Fowler reminds us, "change and evolve over time."

> As we move from one season of our lives to another, in kaleidoscopic fashion the configurations that are our life structures alter in shape and complexity. A

> Christian view of the human vocation suggests that
> partnership with the action of God may be the single
> most fruitful way of finding a principle to orchestrate
> our changing adult life structures.[9]

So now we may have hit the heart of the matter regarding vocation. Vocation denotes that central core of life by which we pull together factors of Creation gifts, social and cultural responsibility, and opportunity for developing gifts to match special needs within one's perceptual field. We can speak then of one's Christian vocation, one's human vocation, or one's "main" vocation and be speaking of something other than job or career. But here the mix thickens, because one's use of career time and energy ultimately becomes a moral and ethical issue before God. Since time and energy are not limitless, the core issue of "vocation" has some serious questions to ask about where we "punch in" and go to work.

## TAPPED ON THE SHOULDER

I met Peter Legner when he was fifteen, when Robbie and I joined with an emerging faith community, the Ginghamsburg United Methodist Church of Tipp City, Ohio, in their annual all-church retreat. It was an amazing week for us, and we came away with several dozen friendships which still thrive. Peter and his friend David wanted to swim late at night in the pool, but regulations required adult supervision for under-age teens and children. I offered to lifeguard, and also talked with Peter about college and the Christian commitment he had made.

A couple of years later, Peter was on board when the clown of a cross country team walked down the aisle of the school bus heading out to a meet, entertaining everybody by pointing out his peers and announcing crazy careers for them.

"Willie here is going to be a garbage collector!"

"John is going to be President of the United States of America!"

When he ambled near Peter, he turned and said, "And everybody knows that Peter is going to be a preacher."

As the clown continued hawking his humor, Peter sat stunned. He had thought of ministry as a possible life calling, but he had no inclination toward it, knowing that it required a call. It was difficult for him to handle other people's sureness about his going into ministry. Significant people in the Ginghamsburg church, quite independent of each other, would stop him to tell him they were sure he was going to be a minister. Peter was not hostile to such an idea, but he was troubled that so many people seemed to know something God was not allowing him to know.

Then it happened. "We went to Jackson, Mississippi, to work with John Perkins at Voice of Calvary ministry. Pastor Mike gave a talk on how 'all Christians are called.' After his talk he asked us to get alone and pray about where God had called us. For the first time it really sunk in that God had called me to be a minister, and the decision facing me was not whether I was called but whether I was going to say 'yes' or 'no.' I couldn't say no to God."

When Peter returned home and told his parents of his sense of calling to pastoral ministry, Peter's mother said, "I've known that for two years." The revelation wasn't a lot of comfort to Peter who already had a backlog of questions for God, but now the question was focused in his own household. "Why had God told everybody else, including the high school clown and his mother, and hadn't let him in on the secret at the beginning?"

Peter's case may have been the call of the community. There was such an incident in the first months of the Christian era. With the exploding good news of the Resurrection transforming people and communities, it became clear that some missionaries were needed. As the Christians huddled, talked, and prayed, "the Holy Spirit said, 'Set apart for me Barnabas and Saul for the work to which I have called them' " (Acts 13:2). We can debate whether the career of "missionary" is vocation or simply job. And we can ask why the community was the instrument of their empowering and of naming their job. Taken in the largest possible sense, however, we might expect that when gifts, needs, and community perceptions are combined, we ought to have a true "vocation" being established.

Indeed, we might suspect my friend Peter, if he announced that he had a private revelation from God that he must be a minister. We might wonder if he was really a competent and stable candidate for such responsibility. The matching up of personal gifts with vocational identity is likely best done outside of the person. Our sense of value and dignity and worth tend to be gathered by the summing up of external transactions. If our peers affirm particular gifts, we then tend to take them seriously. Only people who live in dangerous isolation are likely to have fantastic visions which do not match reality. Among the healthiest of us, we expect an orchestrated match of community perception and of inward openness to the career aspect of vocation.

If vocation is the whole package which matches up who we are—our gifts and how we attach those gifts to needs and opportunities in our world—then we are looking at all of life. Let's highlight some of the elements of vocation.

† I am man or woman. Sexual identity and sex role must be the first self-conscious dimension of vocation. Each of us is able to reconstruct early impressions and formative experiences and words which stretched us to the full stature of our emerging sexuality. And many of us can look back at experiences which caused something in us to wither or die. None of us emerges in our womanhood or our manhood alone.

† I am wife or husband, father or mother. The movement

toward intimacy, marriage, and parenthood figures significantly in our vocation. For males, the movement is often laminated to launching a career and pursuing the life vision. For women the step toward marriage and motherhood is often seen as an alternative to another life vision. But women today are discovering that it is important to have a life vision that includes personal gifts and needs as well as the pursuit of intimacy, marriage, and mothering.

† I am entrepreneur, artist, or engineer. Our vision of what we may be able to do with our particular gifts sets us on the road toward career. When pursued arrogantly, the vision often turns out to be hollow, even though great accomplishment may follow. When laid before the community where respect-based support moves us toward the career that best matches our gifts, the results can be enormously fulfilling.

† I am a steward before God. Here the whole package finally wraps up. Life is a gift—from God. Interests and aptitudes are gifts—from God. Daily survival and energy are gifts—from God. So, as St. Paul could remind us, "Whether we live or die, or whatever we do, we are the Lord's."

While we all search for a sense of purpose in life, it becomes clear that self-grounded, self-made persons are not only dangerous to be around, but are also hollow.

Human vocation is a gift of God, since meaning is linked up to our identities in God's image, and our gifts which are from Him as well. Our jobs, careers, unemployment and disabilities are all ultimately reconcilable with God's calling to the vocation of being human, of being godly, and of doing all of this with integrity.

# W<small>HO?</small>

For none of us lives to himself alone and none of us dies to himself alone. If we live, we live to the Lord, and if we die, we die to the Lord. So, whether we live or die, we belong to the Lord.    Romans 14:7-8

---

## WHERE?

If you did a "vocational inventory" today, how would your sense of identity, of gifts, and of accountability to God who gave them, balance out with your need for integrity and responsibility to God?

## WHAT?

Doodle in the margin here to play with steps you might take to enhance your sense of identity, of gift-use, of accountability to the community and to God.

## WHY?

With whom could you talk this week to open up the questions of your life use and your level of satisfaction that you are doing God's purposes with your energy and time?

## WHEN?

To focus your vocation, ask, "What things most urgently need to be done in my world? How may I attach myself to one of those urgent needs?"

---

# SEVEN

## BREAKING AWAY!

"I'm going to have to call off the wedding because of Mom and Dad." Bud had given Jan the engagement ring nearly a year ago. The date for the wedding was now within two months.

"I'm sorry. I'm all they've got, and they are really threatened by the possibility that I will not be able to support my own home and them."

Bud's father had been unemployed for more than three years—ever since a mild heart attack put him in the hospital. His medical benefits ran almost dry because of the long recuperation, and then his job was gone too. Bud's mother had never worked outside of the home. As an only child, he felt the obligation to support them. He had gotten good work and was able to meet all of the household obligations. Jan had wondered if it might come to this, but their growing attachment and their dreams of a life together with home and children had lessened the possibility that Bud would back out.

But now, the luxury of wife, home, and family faded as Bud considered the impossibility of adding them to his already break-even household. As he turned twenty-three, with the prospect of supporting aging parents for another ten or twenty years, he faced a choice he didn't want to make.

Breaking away from the family of origin to establish a new family unit is the universal experience for humans, from the dawn of history. It remains so in all but highly technological cultures, where we have invented the identity and status of singles, as an intermediate launch pad to marriage or as an alternative lifestyle. The transition from one matrix of intimacy to another intimacy bond that has sufficient energy and resources to launch a new family, is a profound life experience, and an important part of God's curriculum for forming us into mature, responsible people.

When Jesus wanted the call to Christian discipleship put to the acid test, He chose the breaking-away dilemma. "Whoever cannot leave father and mother cannot be My disciple." He also made a remarkable breaking-away statement when people listening to Him assumed that His own mother could preempt His attention.

> While Jesus was still talking to the crowd, His mother and brothers stood outside, wanting to speak to Him. Someone told Him, "Your mother and brothers are standing outside, wanting to speak to You."
>
> He replied, "Who is My mother, and who are My brothers?" Pointing to His disciples, He said, "Here are My mother and My brothers. For whoever does the will of My Father in heaven is My brother and sister and mother."
>
> Matthew 12:46-50

In this chapter we look at the single most universal life experience that faces humans, besides birth and death. Having been nurtured in the parental nest for a whole lifetime, each one faces the prospect of leaving familiar spaces and predictable people. We move on into an uncharted sea of new relationships, and we call another place home. When we marry, we move from the secure and affectionate arms of our parents into the stability of new affection. "I know that I am loved unconditionally," is the peaceable cry of those of us who leave father and mother and fall into the arms of new and ardent love.

Breaking away from family, from home turf, and from predictable security is a major life experience. At issue here, as in all of the experiences we have examined, is our response to God's grace, our ability to trace "the finger of God" in a major life trauma. Leaving home can become an occasion of embracing life, sustained by the deepening grace of God and the perfecting of our appreciation for His presence.

## YOU CAN'T GO HOME AGAIN

Thomas Wolfe wrote the novel, but millions of us have lived it out. Oh, yes, we can make the drive back to the old address, only to find when we get there that home has changed. Relationships are different. The chasm has been fixed.

Rod told us how things actually changed before he left for college. The consultant from Sears had made a visit in June, and by early August there were pink organdy curtains at the windows as the final touch of a room that had been recarpeted and wallpapered to the taste of his fifteen-year-old sister. The two girls would now have separate rooms. So Rod boxed up all of his gear from the closet as the summer waxed warmer. By the middle of August, he was a stranger in space he had known since he was ten. "I knew I wouldn't be coming back to my own space on weekends or holidays. I would sleep on the couch or in the den. In a way it felt good—like it was about time, although I was only turning eighteen as summer ended."

This flushing out of the maturing child is often accompanied by rules which make absolute independence essential. "Go to college if you want to. You're on your own!" are words that have rung in the ears of many emerging adults. Military service attracts some who are dropped from the support of the launching home.

In contrast, the classic case of John Wesley's long dependency on his parents, Samuel and Susanna, demonstrates what can happen when breaking away is postponed. At seventeen, Wesley entered Christ Church College at Oxford University. It was a breaking away at least physically from the parsonage at Epworth. He read widely, played tennis, and participated in the famous Oxford sport—rowing. He reported regular "walking" tours with a "religious friend," identified by some biographers as Sally Kirkham. Sally was evidently engaged to marry someone else. A family friend, a widow named Mrs. Pendarves, provided more friendship, and John Wesley's correspondence with her is sprinkled with light allusions to romance.

But his theological formation was being hammered out in correspondence with his parents. His father was pushing him toward ordination, and would soon urge him to make application for the Anglican vicarage at Epworth and Wroot. Indeed, John Wesley's decision to sail to Georgia as a missionary came at a time which suggests that it was a decisive but non-confrontive way to move away from the control of his parents. He evidently was embarrassed and wanted to escape the unpleasantness occasioned by his failure to apply for the Epworth/Wroot vicarage—a plan his father had proposed and insisted upon.

It is likely that the unhappy missionary adventure in Georgia, while failing in his mission's eyes, actually succeeded in breaking his father's vice grip on his vocational vision and lessening his dependence on his mother's advice. It is easy to speculate that it was his bankruptcy of emotional resource, combined with his romantic misadventure with Sophia Hopkey in Georgia and his sense of failure as an evangelist to the Indians, which created the vacuum which led to his eventual "trusting in Christ and Christ alone" for his salvation. Some developmentalists who have examined the Wesley biographical material suggest that his spiritual grounding which came at thirty-four years of age at a Moravian meeting on Aldersgate Street might have occurred significantly earlier had he broken away from parental dependency earlier.[1]

## BREAKING AWAY WITH FAMILY HELP

We have enjoyed our two sons, John and Mike, from the anticipation of their conception to the present moment. We never
closed up their occupancy rights on the rooms they occupied
before college. And we gave them no proverbial parental shove
to engage adult responsibility and life. But we did give signals
which may have contributed to their courage to try their adult
wings early.

For one thing, the story of our young love and early
marriage was never hidden from them, nor was the pacesetting
pattern of my parents. Dad had negotiated Mother's hand out of
the Royer household south of Clay City, Indiana. With full
consent and having just turned eighteen, Dad drove Mother to
Danville, Illinois in October of 1925 to marry in a civil ceremo-
ny. Church weddings were simply not a cultural phenomenon in
their tradition.

Marrying with the enthusiastic support of Royers and
Joys in families a thousand miles apart, they shuttled between
Kansas and Indiana during my childhood, and I felt richly loved
by uncles, aunts, and cousins at both ends of U.S. Highway 40.

When Robbie and I fell in love, it was clear that both
sets of parents were only slightly less excited than we were with
the prospects of marriage in 1948, before I turned twenty and
while Robbie was eighteen. I am reporting this to suggest that
in the twentieth century the launching of young adult children
into intimacy and marriage stands as one of the more wholesome settings in which breaking away occurs. When the model
has been established in previous generations, the unspoken curriculum of the late teens becomes, "When and with whom will I
establish my distinct identity as an adult?" Our boys breathed it
in the atmosphere of the home and the frequent contacts with

grandparents.

"I wish we could give our sons the same good start we got," Robbie mused. "When your folks gave us their new Plymouth as a surprise wedding gift and then paid the insurance on it until we graduated from college, that really took the pressure off and let us both stay in school."

"We could do that," I speculated. And we agreed that we would make it a family tradition. I remember when we announced our plan to the boys, "We've decided that we don't want you to get your heart set on having your own car while you are in high school or college. We will try to keep a couple of cars around to furnish you any transportation you need. Then, just as my parents gave us a new car when we were married, we'll do the same for you—or when you graduate from college, whichever comes first. It will be a full-sized, four-door Chevy, or the equivalent."

The way I phrased the plan may have tilted them toward marriage before they finished college. I had not consciously framed the offer to bias it toward early marriage, and they never hinted that my proposition set wedding bells ringing in their heads. But we bought new Chevy rolling stock for John in 1972, just after he had turned twenty, and for Mike four years later—three months after he turned twenty.

Besides the new automobiles, we pledged to pay college expenses at a proportional rate through graduation, for our new daughters-in-law as well as our sons, and to keep up the car insurance until they finished college level work.

When we moved to Kentucky, we had an opportunity to buy two houses on the same property. One, with the apartment we had occupied in seminary days ourselves, became our launching house for the boys and their families, in quick succession.

On one occasion we got resistance from our daughter-in-law when we asked for the car insurance premium notice we knew had arrived, since ours was due as well. I broke down the barriers by saying, "Let me tell you that there is no obligation to us that goes with the money. My parents did this for us when we were in college. We are doing it for you. You will never repay us, but we will be interested to see what you are doing about launching your new baby twenty years from now." She accepted the explanation. "When you put it that way, I guess you can pay the car insurance."

There was a grand celebration when the final support strings were cut. That same daughter-in-law told us enthusiastically after they had moved into their very own home, "The day I saw our name in the Lexington phone directory, I knew we had grown up."

Robbie and I have been pleased—but we expected exactly what we got—with both of our sons coming of age and taking responsibility for themselves, marrying, and launching families. We knew that if we could stick with them through the adolescent years, eventually they would hit rotation and leave the runway our home had provided, and would literally be airborne and on their own. So we endorsed their vision, affirmed their responsible autonomy, and began taking hands off long before we got the signal that they no longer depended on our day-by-day emotional and economic support.

I had been teaching David Ausubel's satellization model of the family[2] for two or three years before John came to the end of high school. The various options in that model had warmed my heart, and I saw illustrations of the basic model in our life experience.

† Satellization. In early childhood, the well-satellized child cannot distinguish between the self and the parents. When a kid gives the signal that family festivities, family excursions, and family decisions are the "best there are," you know satellization is occurring.

"My daddy has more money than your daddy has!" our

four-year-old Mike taunted his friend Evon Horton. The issue was laughable, given the poverty level incomes of their denominational servant fathers at that time. But the debate raged.

Eventually, Eva, Evon's mother, heard the argument end, as Mike framed the winning punch, "Well, your daddy may have more money than my daddy, but my daddy has Texas money!" Poor bewildered Evon didn't know how to combat such status and role. But Mike had been born in Dallas and was still nurtured in a Texas cultural environment which, in many ways, is virtually indestructible.

Ausubel claims that the well-satellized child predicts well, for eventually spinning into orbit on a new identity which will highly resemble the family of origin.

† Desatellization. When the kid breaks away, there are typically some painful and frightening moments. Parents get the idea that the nest is breaking up; the insecurity of a shift in roles and status can be very traumatic. Parents often feel rejected when their children begin to show high admiration for new models, often teachers and coaches. Yet, without such temporary surrogate parents, the desatellization period may be characterized by some role and status experimentation.

Erik Erikson referred to this adolescent crucible as being torn between the desire to establish a clear identity and the pull, toward identity diffusion or experimentation. The pressures of teen culture pull many emerging adults into potentially deadly identity experimentation, involving high speed automobiles, dangerous and addictive substances, and sexual behaviors which leave long-term consequences if they are lucky, and disease and death if they are not. Often the new models are media personalities who are too removed from reality to be useful, and too flawed to serve the children's needs for a temporary model.

Genuinely heroic desatellization sometimes occurs in high integrity people whose leaving home is sudden and largely free from a mounting appetite to "be on my own." David Ellis, whose family friendship we have enjoyed for two generations before his birth, told his spiritual formation group of his experience of breaking away.

"My father and one of his best friends drove me from New Jersey to Greenville College. We stopped overnight enroute, putting us into Greenville after a day and a half of driving. I hadn't realized that the two men would unload me and leave immediately to start the long trip home. When my father said that it was time for them to go, I hugged him and said good-bye. Then I watched from the window of my residence hall as they piled into the car and drove off. It hit me suddenly that this was really happening, and that for the first time in my life I was really alone. Since it was Labor Day weekend and most students would not arrive for a couple of days, my sense of isolation was sharpened by the emptiness of the dormitory. I remember going into my room to unpack and feeling abandoned. I didn't phone home for several weeks. I had this sense that I was going to have to grieve and get some healing for this lost childhood of mine. So I guess I put myself in isolation from my family so I could enter a new phase of my life."

† Resatellization. Here is the "coming home." The now launched young adult will tend to survive the desatellization. The well-satellized prepubsecent child tends to resist most of the "identity diffusion and experimentation" pull during adolescence. Even when pulled into the confusing malestrom of peer pressure and media seduction, the nicely satellized child most often stabilizes and "returns home" to values and behavior very like those of the formative family matrix. Ausubel gives comfort to those of us who have clung to the ancient proverb: "Train a child in the way he should go, and when he is old he will not turn from it" (Proverbs 22:6).

† Nonsatellization. Ausubel warns that if for any reason the very young child rejects the intimate identification with parents—the spontaneous and delightful satellization experi-

ence—there will be trouble. The nonsatellizer gives early signals that it is not "at home" with the parents. There is consistent resistance to parental affection, to activities with the parent, and the parental affirmation. The kid seems turned outward, eager to do violence at home and outside the home as well. While some abused children cling to parents and virtually overdepend on them, some are so alienated that they sense that they will have to be survivors, that "there is no help here." Other nonsatellizing children show up among the hyperkinetic group which need special diagnosis and long-term therapy if they are to avoid the antisocial and probably tragic consequences of the nonsatellized child when the adolescent and young adult years are negotiated.

## *SURROGATE PARENTS—MENTORS*

During the resatellization process, Ausubel's model of adolescent development predicts that some temporary hookups will occur between respected mentors outside of the family. Those relationships tend to be as unself-consciously idolatrous as is the toddler's naked imitation of the parent. The emerging young adult tends to pick up ways of speaking, thinking, valuing, and choosing which seem to be carbon copies of these strangers to the parents. It can be a time of enormous threat to parents, since the idolatry is so visible and without shame.

We lived through a siege of the mentor idolatry when each of our sons hit seventh grade. We listened to endless quotations of the special teacher and the admired coach. It was clear that the real "clout" had shifted to these surrogate parents—these mentors of our boys. We took a lot of comfort in their choice of mentors. And we realized that we ourselves in youth ministry had become the temporary "landing dock" for several teens who were on their way into the adult orbit, but wanted to refuel at our inflight center of attention and affection.

John and Sherry Benson chilled us to the bone one Sunday morning before some of these "breaking away" patterns had fallen into a decent theory or model. They said, "We want you to know that we pray for you every morning, and we pray earnestly. Right now we have two sons who think you can do no wrong, and if anything happened by which you let them down, we don't know if we could pick up the pieces."

Surrogates, mentors, and the objects of young adult idolatry don't ask for the admiration—it just comes with the territory of any kind of community. We need to look more intentionally at the pattern of such dependencies in the midst of launching into independence, to see if we can prepare ourselves to do a better job of being there when kids need to refuel with mentors.

Mentors serve as a relatively objective, outside sounding board to allow the young to evaluate their life experiences, to reshape their naive dreams, and to find healing without humiliation. And we need to be able to describe such emerging "modeling on a respected model" in healthy terms, to identify positive characteristics of such a relationship, and to train ourselves to "move with the kid" so the relationship does not become symbiotic—stuck in an unhealthy "idolatry and idol" syndrome.

A young adult relationship with a mentor is healthy when both people can identify that a special relationship is forming; when the senior member can describe the probable duration of a healthy launch—normally three to eight years; and when the senior member can coach the junior member into a relationship that is based on mutual respect and that leads to lifelong friendship. Such a relationship looks very much like a healthy parent-child relationship.

Unhealthy mentor relationships that lead to idolatry are consistently destructive. They tend to be characterized by

† the overdependence of the emerging adult on the senior

† an excessive pleasure displayed by the senior at control-

ling and exploiting the younger admirer

† signs that either the junior or the senior member of the dyad is maintaining the relationship, and refusing to let growth and healthy change occur by which the young adult might become autonomous and even exceed the competence and the reputation of the mentor.

Mentors are a special gift of the Creator. Every kid deserves to take the measure of "what it means to be an adult in my culture." The best bred young adults are programmed to be open to outside models and images of maturity during the mid to late teen years. And the most emotionally impoverished children in your community may be transformed during that vulnerable time, if they "hitch their wagon to the star" of some high-fidelity warm person who is willing to do a bit of surrogate parenting for a few years. Desatellization is indeed magic, even though it is full of threats for all parents.

It is pretty clear that St. Paul was the mentor of young Timothy in his growth into responsible and disciplined Christian adulthood. Paul affirmed Timothy's worth, warned him to turn a deaf ear to people who devalued his youthfulness, and reminded him of his faithful mother and grandmother. Such affirmation of the launching home is a critical test of any surrogate to whom the emerging adult attaches while breaking away. Consider the constructive, put-it-in-the-best-light-possible mentoring in a few samples of St. Paul's writings to Timothy:

"To Timothy, my true son in the faith" (1 Timothy 1:2).

"Timothy, my son, I give you this instruction in keeping with the prophecies once made about you, so that by following them you may fight the good fight" (1:18).

"Don't let anyone look down on you because you are young, but set an example for the believers in speech, in life, in love, in faith, and in purity. Until I come, devote yourself to the public reading of Scripture, to preaching and to teaching. Do not neglect your gift, which was given you through a pro-

phetic message when the body of elders laid their hands on you"
(4:12-14).

"To Timothy, my dear son . . . Recalling your tears, I
long to see you, so that I may be filled with joy. I have been
reminded of your sincere faith, which first lived in your grandmother, Lois and in your mother, Eunice, and I am persuaded,
now lives in you also. For this reason, I remind you to fan into
flame the gift of God, which is in you through the laying on of
my hands. For God did not give us a spirit of timidity, but a
spirit of power, of love and of self-discipline" (2 Timothy 1:2,
4-7).

## LETTING GO: THE OTHER SIDE OF BREAKING AWAY

It is ironic that the two people on earth who are most admired,
even idolized, become the adversaries of the adolescent years.
The so-called generation gap often refers to the separation impulse, the demagnetizing of the parent-child bond, that comes
with the arrival of sexual ripening. It would be easy to link the
phenomenon with sexual chemistry—the chemistry of the brain
during the flooding of the fresh supply of hormones, for example. But we can also regard it as God's way of guaranteeing that
our children will, indeed, leave home and establish their own
nests someplace else with appropriate partners of their own. So
let us coin a comforting verse for parents, "Be not dismayed
when desatellization occurs; for this cause did you bring these
children into the world."

Sexual ripening is an intrinsic, often unnamed life crisis.
It signals the young person that fertility has arrived. But it also
confronts the awful truth: it is not good for a mature, fertile
human to be alone. First signs of pubescence often show in the
growth spurt of some change in genital or secondary sex physical configuration such as the appearance of body hair. But virtu-

ally simultaneously, the kid locks the bathroom door and makes peace with the face and the body in the mirror. Questions of identity and worth flood the mind: Who will respect me? Who would want me for the rest of my life? How can I make myself more acceptable to myself, let alone my peers?

The security of the locked bathroom is symbolic of a deeper need of privacy. The kid who blurted out all kinds of candid questions and opinions and who kept no secrets at all—even when Christmas and birthday secrets were on the line—now clams up.

"Where have you been?"

"Out."

"Who were you with?"

"Nobody."

"Did you have fun?"

"Naw."

Thomas Gordon would run out of gas in a conversation like this, but he would at least make an effort with something like: "I get it. You went looking for some old friends. You found a couple of them, and talked for the last two hours. But mainly you need to have some space and some secrets of your own, so you would like for me not to expect you to tell me every little detail like you did when you were younger."

"You got it. Thanks!"

And we might as well "get it," because we brought them into the world to set them free. We had about thirteen to fifteen years to cultivate them to be responsible, sensitive to human feelings and to the truth. From here on, we are dealing with emerging adults, and we are the first to know that they are, indeed, grown up.

Breaking away never looked better to Robbie and me than when we saw it showing up in our sons. And we celebrated a thousand thanks to God for giving us parents who read the signals, though they had never read psychology. We suspect that families which bloody themselves in emotional violence during the launching years with their children may have had less confidence based on their own launching. If their own breaking away left them with pain, guilt, and unresolved anger toward parents, they are likely to replicate that guilt-anger-pain formula when their children are ready to go. However, we have also seen people who have been bruised by their own launching and yet are able to make an intentional and orderly Christian launching of their own children into adulthood and marriage.

# W HO?

Train up a child in the way he should go and when he is old he will not turn from it.

Proverbs 22:6

## WHERE?

Rewrite your own breaking away. How do you wish it had been different. Who would have benefited most—you or your parents and mentors?

## WHAT?

List three people you know are now struggling with issues of breaking away, of establishing their own identity. Who is "there" for them to stabilize them as they start down the runway into adulthood?

## WHY?

Identify one actual blessing that came to you from some turbulence or pain while breaking away. Even your own rebellion can be turned by God's grace into something good.

## WHEN?

Make a note to call a parent or a young adult who is caught in the breaking away territory, and offer encouragement.

# EIGHT

## DEALING WITH PAIN

Clive Staples Lewis is not only *The Apostle to the Skeptics,* as Chad Walsh has noted; he is also a rare bridge between traditional Anglo-Catholics and the larger Christian world. Indeed, he is a darling among evangelicals. Who of us has not read his *Mere Christianity* or the lovely set of children's novels meant to be appreciated by adults, *The Chronicles of Narnia?*

I name C. S. Lewis here, not simply because so many of us love him and his view of radical Christian faith. And I bypass for now his reputation as a philologist and English scholar— though I went literally to the roots of Nat Whilk Clerk, his careful pseudonym used first to cloak his boyhood poetry published in the *London Times* and later to cover his profound grief at the loss of Joy Davidson, his wife taken late. But I name him for the obvious ways that pain was C. S. Lewis' curriculum. I want to focus on his pain across decades. His story of personal grief over the loss of Joy was, of course, the pseudonymously written *A Grief Observed.* But he had wrestled with a theology of suffering in both *The Problem of Pain* and in key elements of *Miracles.*

We sometimes imagine that we would love to dance with wisdom, to have great insights, to be a persuasive teacher. But we rarely have a corresponding appetite for pain. Yet pain is the crucible from which insight and wisdom emerge.

C. S. Lewis lost his mother to a progressive illness which evidently extended across his sixth, seventh, and eighth years of life. In one breath he remembers his world of imagination and his search for "joy." That search was not for pleasure or happiness, but consisted simply of an awareness that he was on a quest—that yearning and desire for meaning. But in the other breath—literally within two pages of his autobiography, *Surprised by Joy*—Lewis describes the horrendous loss and emptiness that came with the loss of his mother. One night he was sick, and he cried because of his own physical discomfort. But he cried more because his mother would not—could not—leave her sickbed and come to nurture him.

His mother's death ushered in his first experience of religion, but it was oriented toward magic. God was "neither Saviour nor Judge, but merely a magician." He hardly noticed when his prayers for his mother's magical healing were not effective. He was used to "things not working."

Life then centered in boarding schools for young Lewis. At Chartres, a confused but benevolent matron provided the unsettling affirmation by which young Lewis was ceasing to say, "I believe" and more cautiously saying, "One does feel." It was there that he "ceased to be a Christian." This unbelief was to follow Lewis through World War I and a battlefield injury, through university years, and into his career. Eventually he would declare, "All religions, that is all mythologies, to give them their proper name, are merely human invention."

Lewis' undoing as an agnostic came, ironically, through "academics." He almost by accident picked up George MacDonald's *Phantastes*. As he devoured it, the author's appeal to honesty linked up with his own yearning for "joy." He reports that his imagination "was baptized" that night. But the rest of him, "not surprisingly, took longer."

Reading Chesterton, another literary giant then unknown to Lewis, he was magnetically held. "I liked him for his goodness." The ideas and images in Chesterton linked up with a guileless man named Johnson, a wartime friend whom Lewis had found amazing for his innocence during his own apostasy of values. So, Lewis reports, he began to imitate Chesterton and Johnson, since imitation is the only response one can bring when the heart is empty.

Finally, "in the Trinity term of 1929," Lewis became a theist, knelt, and prayed. He reports that it was a conversion to God, but that he was not yet a Christian. Indeed, he describes himself as "the most dejected and reluctant convert in all of England." He was, he says, like the Jews, believing in God, but not yet concerned with the deity, the resurrection, and with the reward of heaven. Indeed, he worries in his autobiography that he was never able to see "how a preoccupation with that subject at the outset could fail to corrupt the whole thing. . . . God was to be obeyed simply because He was God."

His Christian conversion came sometime later as Lewis was being driven to Whipsnade one bright morning. "When we set out I did not believe that Jesus Christ is the Son of God, and when we reached the zoo, I did. Yet, I had not exactly spent the journey in thought. . . . It was . . . like a man, after long sleep, still lying motionless in bed, becomes aware that he is now awake." It is that experience he describes as being "surprised by joy."

Lewis explores his pilgrimage in search of joy, and ends his life story with an amazing report. "To tell you the truth, the subject (of joy) has lost nearly all interest for me since I became a Christian." He likens that inner hunger for meaning, the thirst for satisfaction, to a road pointer one might see when lost in the woods. The lost hikers huddle around the signpost in the forest; but once they find the road and are "passing signposts every few miles, [they do] not stop and stare." Indeed, the relentless and urgent push to get on to the destination makes all the pointers and signposts turn pale by comparison to the reality: living in pursuit of God whom we have seen in Jesus, and stretching to obey the summons of the hunger and thirst for righteousness. This is "meaning making" beyond joy.[1]

# LEARNING TO SUFFER

As you read this chapter, I am eager for you to trace your own pilgrimage, to see the roles which grief, trouble, pain, even doubt, agnosticism and despair may have played in bringing you to your present good estate of faith. These life experiences are so unpleasant that we recoil at the prospect that they may be part of the real curriculum of human development and destiny. Indeed, we are eager to avoid them wherever possible. This avoidance is part of healthy human aspiration for positive and constructive experience. But our character and our spirit are dwarfed if we push them quickly aside, even deny the reality of the pilgrimage of anguish, and pretend that life consists only of rosy, constructive, and painless tranquility.

We are masters at avoiding pain. But we are even more gifted in putting on a facade which denies that we are now or ever have suffered. This deception is the most destructive of all of our devices. At the surface level it reduces us to liars, while deep within, we burrow to hide the very stuff which might have produced greatness: honesty, sensitivity, and a profound authority from our own curriculum of painful experience.

The Religious Education Association commissioned a Gallup Poll study of adult faith. So, in a telephone survey conducted between March 18 and 31, 1985, the Princeton-based Gallup agency did extensive interviews with 1,042 adults. They reported that changes in faith were significantly related to "periods of transition and crisis" in the adults' lives. The crises most often mentioned were long periods of loneliness, a conscious decision to leave one's present church or faith community, undergoing professional counseling or therapy for emotional difficulty, the birth of a child (for both fathers and mothers), divorce, and being born again.[2]

To these I would add other common experiences—dealing with the terminal illness and death of a spouse or a child, abuse, rejection, and neglect. There are personal and internal struggles—unbelief which slides into agnosticism and flirts with atheism, loneliness which paves the path into reclusive withdrawal, and depression which progressively eliminates options for reentering meaningful living.

It is depressing even to read such a list. Unlike modern pagan religions of prosperity and elitism, virtually all ancient religions assigned an important role to pain and trouble, in relation to achieving maturity or the golden end for the human pilgrimage. Indeed, Aeschylus, classical Greek dramatist, caught the idea clearly in these lines from *Agamemnon:* "Wisdom comes alone through suffering. . . . Justice so moves that those only learn who suffer."

We read Jesus wrongly if we imagine that He has special affinity with the affluent. Indeed, Jesus read His inaugural statement from the pain-laced words of Isaiah (Luke 4). The statement was radically focused on people in anguish.

The Spirit of the Sovereign Lord is on Me,
 because the Lord has anointed Me
 to preach good news to the poor.
He has sent Me to bind up the brokenhearted,
 to proclaim freedom for the captives
 and release for the prisoners,
 to proclaim the year of the Lord's favor
 and the day of vengeance of our God,
To comfort all who mourn,
 and to provide for those who grieve in Zion—
 to bestow on them a crown of beauty instead of ashes,
 the oil of gladness instead of mourning,
 and a garment of praise instead of a spirit of despair.
They will be called oaks of righteousness,
 a planting of the Lord
 for the display of His splendor.   Isaiah 61:1-3

So committed was Jesus to the meeting of pain and righteousness that He never "hit a person when they were down." He confronted wickedness in religious people, but never condemned a hurting person, however immoral. Indeed, when Matthew wanted to describe the way Jesus ministered to the sick and the hurting, he quoted Isaiah 42:1-4.

> Here is My Servant whom I have chosen,
>      the one I love, in whom I delight;
> I will put my Spirit on Him,
>      and He will proclaim justice to the nations.
> He will not quarrel or cry out;
>      no one will hear His voice in the streets.
> A bruised reed He will not break,
>      and a smoldering wick He will not snuff out,
>      till He leads justice to victory.
> In His name will the nations put their hope.
>                                      Matthew 12:18-21

## AN ACCOUNTABILITY NETWORK

This book is dedicated to a dozen men who have been my accountability network now for ten years. I first met them in campus brown-bag support group sessions when they were students. There is almost nothing we have not disclosed to each other. Within the last twelve months, for example, we have processed major chunks of life curriculum in this primary accountability network.

† We wrestled along with David as he contemplated his gifts, his healing from childhood anguish, and what these emerging sensitivities dictate about his career.

† We hung on to Rick as he took an official leave of absence from the ordaining body, in order to "make some meaning" of the inner-city challenge confronting him.

✝    We listened to Ben as he traced feelings of present inferiority back into childhood, and we embraced the competent self we consistently discover him to be.

✝    We reflected with Ken as he bumped personal and professional integrity up against the realities of his present opportunities.

✝    We surrounded Alan as he walked the uncharted road to his wife's grave, after her battle with breast cancer.

✝    We listened to the early midlife juggling of career and ministry options with which Daryl wrestles.

✝    We celebrated Don's survival from a head-on car-truck collision.

✝    We reflected with Rob on his long-term vulnerability to compulsive ambition.

✝    We celebrated Ike's progress in winning the battle over his authoritarian impulses and felt his struggle with the offers of positions with increased power.

✝    We held on to Karl as he went through withdrawal from compulsive pastoral success tendencies and sustained the shock of intentionally becoming a church planter.

✝    We affirmed Greg's priorities, including their precedence over our meeting schedules.

✝    We walked with Dean through major personal and professional adaptations which came with the turf of a new pastoral appointment.

✝    And they listened and struggled with me, as I face the seventh decade of life and must, yet again, review priorities for my use of time and energy in the face of increasing demands. I am more radically Christian because of these men and their gifts of candor and support. It is sobering to know that I cannot hide myself from them.

To get into some universal principles for dealing with painful life experience, I want to unfold some of the scenarios of pain I have seen firsthand. These living anecdotes are representative of the anguish which lies concealed within most of us. But what you will reflect on as we listen and look may give you some first clues about how beauty may, indeed, be formed out of ashes.

## IN WHOSE IMAGE?

There are few chunks of pain more troublesome than those which disrupt the family during childhood. Take Roger's case. He grew up wild, he says, on the streets of Los Angeles. His parents' marriage was turning into a divorce, and with their preoccupation with their own problems, Roger's daily life was literally on the streets. Even in extensive therapy as an adult, he has been unable to dredge up typical childhood memories. Something was frozen back there which set even the most precious memories into hardened glacial material. But there was a grandmother who corraled him as a young teenager and dragged him to church. That's how Jesus got hold of him. And that's how he turned up eventually at seminary.

He has worked now for several decades building a beautiful castle of adult faith and a significant career on the core of a painfully damaged childhood. But his honesty with peers and with mentors has been Roger's "anchor." The shattered core of his childhood has left a spackled pattern across adolescence, then marriage, and into his parenting and career years. From time to time he worries that the fragile structure may break and he may run wild to the streets again. But the shattered crystal interior is beginning to throw muted shadows of beauty on his life. His work with people in pain and trouble is showing the mark of authority. Instead of feeling the follicles raise in fear at the encroaching story of some teen's collapsing world, he now finds empathy awakening. His strength has been formed from weakness.

Gene is another friend whose family support collapsed.

He phoned me on Commencement morning to ask, "Who is sitting with Robbie? Would it be okay if Donna sat with her? We don't have any family here today." It was a small piece of loneliness, so small, in fact, that it would have gone unnoticed as families crowded the campus to celebrate with more than two hundred graduates. So Robbie sat with Gene's wife. We also took them to dinner and acted late to be "family to them." Today Gene and Donna are so well healed from the early rejection Gene received from his father that they are able to take their turn at "parenting" the very man who so resented Gene's teenage conversion. Gene's Dad was angered that Gene's brothers followed him to Christian faith, and refused to endorse help in Gene's college and seminary education in pursuit of his vision.

What do you say to the vacuum that developed for Roger and for Gene? The family is God's normal curriculum for learning trust and reliability—both root images of God. Roger and Gene have reached out in radical honesty to other people. They have had to deal with compulsive needs which were rooted in the early pain of loneliness for parental support. But their early losses were not the end of the world. If you are lucky enough today to be among the thousands of people ministered to by servants of God like Roger and Gene, you will be able to celebrate the "beauty for ashes" and the "oil of joy for mourning" exchange they have made for their pain.

In cases like these, it would be easy to predict adult disaster. A fatalistic or deterministic view would see Roger as hopelessly flawed. And Gene's compulsive tendencies would predict probably competitive and destructive effects. But both of them found outside help. Can you hear the echo of a promise from the Psalms? "When father and mother forsake you, then the community of faith may become your family."

Marshall McLuhan's principle applies here: "Nothing is inevitable if you are willing to contemplate what is happening."

And you could bring the issue closer to Roger and Gene by observing a first principle: *God has created you with an appetite for order and health, so take seriously the appetite to reach out and find the relationships to fill the vacuums in your life.* What do father-absent people need? What do the rejected need? The answers are so obvious that we sometimes forget to even ask the question.

When we look at the primary curriculum of the father and mother relationship, it is clear that a child's sense of worth, order, and stability is formed right there. Roger, with a surge of healthy survival instinct, took to the streets. He was a survivor, but with substantial emotional and affective damage.

A second principle emerges: *Healing comes through finding replacement relationships and experiences to "back fill" what was damaged or lost.* I was one of Roger's mentors, but at first hardly detected his appeal for "refathering."

"I've had the only course from you that I can crowd into my degree. But I would like to know more about you. Could I spend an hour or two with you every week this year anyway?" Indeed, the "spiritual formation" or "support groups" with which I have worked consistently across the years were really established long ago as my response to Roger. But I may not have met his needs well. I was so uneasy with his threatening request that I asked for time. Two days later I told him I would welcome a "brown bag lunch hour" in the dining commons if he could round up a couple of additional students. I suppose I saw safety in numbers. I was baffled that spring and all the next year that Roger seemed marginalized by the growing group. His needs were better met one-on-one, so we managed to find other exclusive times. We gardened side by side that summer. He and our sons meshed in age and he enjoyed some sense of being adopted into our family and household activities. He found a place where the pain of that "shattering core" could be cried out in primal anguish; the support of surrogate and mentor became more like the respect and care of a brother.

## *WILL I EVER SING AGAIN?*

My Grandma Joy said she wouldn't. She had survived a Model-A car crash at an intersection where her young son drove straight through into an embankment. She would carry her scars for life. But the worst news imaginable arrived like a bullet: her oldest son was dead, a drowning victim, in the Solomon River near Salina.

There were months when Grandma did not sing. She did not sing at home, and that was understandable. But I, sitting with Grandma and Grandpa Joy in my favorite pew at church, could not imagine why she could not sing along with all of us there. However, Grandma grieved well, because she could talk freely about her pain. Many folks today avoid the territory of grief. Some traditions mask the grief with alcohol, even partying to kill the instant sense of loss.

Alan, the only hero in our accountability network to do hand-to-hand combat with a death in his own household, is going to sing again. Two months following his wife's death, we got an update on his and the girls' progress. His grieving is conspicuously wholesome. He is systematically studying and reflecting on his journey with Idabelle into the valley of the shadow of death.

I have not felt much like writing anyone. Not until today have I finally gotten the motivation to get things moving. . . . I am perpetually thankful for friends who understand that this is an appointed season. I did not choose it, nor would I have chosen it. Even if we do not choose winter, it doesn't mean winter will be shorter or warmer. I am like a fish out of water. I flop around with a burst of enthusiasm every now and then, thinking I am making great progress. Then I find that I am still out of water. So I

watch the water, knowing that sometime I will get back in.
I am living under the Mercy.

So the third principle emerges: *Any form of denial in dealing with pain postpones or badly deforms grief.* "The mortician says we should not open the casket," a grief-stricken parent reports. But it will be crucial for those who loved the most to come to a visual separation from the beloved person now lost to death.

"Did you have a chance to hold your stillborn baby?"

"No. The doctor asked us if we wanted to hold her, but we didn't know whether that would be right, so we didn't." And their grief is complicated by the memory that they were unable to deliver their best affection—the gesture of accepting touch—to their lost baby.

"Call the doctor and get a prescription," is the thoughtful intervention of well-intentioned members of the family, but masking grief with chemicals may come at a higher price than any of us want to pay. In most cases, the absolute commitment of trusted relatives and friends is more health-giving than the artificial relief from tranquilizers.

"Did you name the baby?" I asked of a maturing couple, still grieving their secretly aborted premarital baby when they were seventeen.

"No, and we thought that when we got married and had children, we would finally be able to forget the abortion," they said, "but instead it only gets worse. Our two young children are living reminders that we had another baby and killed it."

"I recommend that you give it a code name known only to the two of you. You need to have a fixed point and image around which to focus your grief. I want to release you from your guilt, but your grief will ripen you and make you safe and helpful to others for the rest of your life, if you will deal with it honestly with each other whenever it surfaces."

Beyond denial comes a fourth principle: *Naming the pain*

*blunts its power to hurt and to control.* We often are eager to tiptoe around the specific event or issue. It is common for a spouse or a parent to seal off the memory of the person lost to death or other painful and permanent separation. In those cases, not only is the loss denied, but the positive memories are forfeited by veiled references to time or place. For example, "Before June of '69 we used to camp at the Dunes," is a way of avoiding the specificity of the cancer death of fifteen-year-old Del. We even tend to speak to God in generalities, as if He could not possibly see the specifics in His all-seeing scanning of eternity and space. Just as the old Hebrew concept of naming and therefore controlling defined the human's relationship to the birds, animals, and vegetation at Creation, so also does the specific naming of anguish put us in control over our circumstances, even those that are tragic.

What do we say to death? When it comes slowly blinking its flashing lights for months, even years, we can do much of our grieving before the separating knife is dropped. But sudden death gives us no such warning, no homework to finish before the test.

I was on the receiving end when a young but confident pastor sat with four of us in the day-after daze of dealing with the sudden death of a precious twenty-one-year-old prince in an auto crash. "I want to tell you," the pastor began after he had formed us into a circle of bonded hands, "that whatever you are feeling today is right. Feelings of anger, despair, even resentment are all acceptable. You see, God did not create death. Death is always an intruder. Death intruded into God's perfect creation, so God joins you in your emotions which resist death. And Jesus came to die and to put an end, finally, to the power of death. We saw it in the Resurrection. Now, let's pray." And he opened the door for us to say something coherent directly to death. Grief well sheathed in God's grace is a means of meaning-making and maturing. Indeed, if we can grieve well, there is likely no other means so powerful.

## *HELP MY UNBELIEF!*

Jane booked me into her community college residence hall to talk on "pair bonding" for the second consecutive campus visit in a row. A month later she surprised me by driving to my campus to keep an appointment made through the secretary. I had, in fact, not connected her name on the secretary's pink sheet with the lectures she had invited me to do with her dormitory women.

"Well, are you surprised?"

"A little, but I'm glad to see you. What is going on?"

"You probably thought I had you come to lecture in my dorm because I was concerned about my girls. And I am. But it was also because I am confused."

Jane then unfolded a life story around these elements: She was presently sleeping with a very demanding, selfish man on every holiday and day off. They had been relating sexually for seven years, with marriage always dangled slightly ahead of the present moment. She was promiscuous during junior high and senior high days before entering into this virtual live-in arrangement while in college. And before that, her father had used her sexually between the ages of nine and fifteen.

"I can't imagine how I ever got into your 'bonding stuff,'" she went on. "It is so religious, and I only go through the motions of religion. I've been to church all my life, but I don't remember a time when it was honest, unless it was when I was really very young. But you make so much sense, and I know that you are right. It's just that I can't live a lie all the time and be a Christian too."

"Good point. But you ceased living a lie about thirty minutes ago when you told the truth."

"I can't believe I'm doing that either. And it is really

strange that I'm talking to you, because you are about the age of my father, and I wouldn't tell him the truth for anything. In fact, I don't tell my boyfriend the truth anymore. I'm really not your basic truthful person. Except with these girls. I can be honest with them. They don't know about my boyfriend, of course. I have to live a lie to them on that."

Jane had defined the root of her unbelief and her deception. The rule is clear: *Unfinished business from childhood tends to predict unbelief and deception today and tomorrow. The sins of the fathers rob the faith of children and children's children.* But since Jane could name the idol, it lost its power. Honesty embraced at the smallest level—her disclosure to me—opened the door for integrity to begin to seep back into all of her life.

As we deal with a damaged childhood, with desperate grief, or the practical atheism of going through religious motions without belief, we construct alternatives to doubt, deception, depression, blind grief, and rejection and desertion from childhood. It remains for us to see what our present pain and suffering may present us as trophies for our persistent pilgrimage "through many dangers, toils, and snares."

# W HO?

Unless I see the nail marks in His hands and put my finger where the nails were, and put my hand into His side, I will not believe it!
I do believe; help me overcome my unbelief!
John 20:25; Mark 9:24

## WHERE?

Where have you put the hard questions you need to lay before God? Is there someone you need to embrace and tell, with Joseph, "Do not be angry with yourselves for selling me here, because it was to save lives that God sent me ahead of you"?

## WHAT?

Can you pull your doubts and squelched anger or pain "out of the varnish" where you buried them, and let them honestly rise in anguished prayer? A glossed, plastic faith is less honest than infantile naivete, and closes the door to maturing faith.

## WHY?

If Jesus has called us to explore and to know the truth, then He is calling us to come forward with the real questions of our lives, since at the core of them we will find Him, for He is truth!

## WHEN?

Today, of course. Buried resentments, questions unasked because they seemed to flirt with doubt, may produce cancer of the soul. At best, they limit our effectiveness as bearers of the image of God.

# NINE

## BECOMING FRIENDS

Emmet hitchhiked several hundred miles to begin college. He had heard the president of the school speak at a family camp only weeks before. No one in his family had been beyond eighth grade except Emmet, and he had just recently graduated from high school. He arrived without application forms completed or a formal admission.

"How did you hear of this college?" the admissions officer asked.

"Mr. Hale spoke at a summer camp where I visited for one day. I wrote down the day school was to open. It seemed like I should be here."

By an unusual providence, Emmet was ushered into the president's office and the magical timing brought the two men face to face. Dr. Hale cleared the way for his immediate admission; and since a work-study program was an obvious necessity to broker the bill, Emmet found himself looking at campus employment. President Hale sent through a request that the young man be assigned, if possible, to a maintenance task which included after-hours cleaning of the presidential suite and of the guest space which was a part of the president's home.

Today, a generation later, Emmet is president of that college. You can fill in the blanks. The early contact, the intermediate years of study and work, and Dr. Hale's growing sense that Emmet had special gifts—all of these were the trajectory which led from vagrant freshman to college president.

Emmet's story is typical of so many—young person is befriended by mentor or parent, young person learns the trade and eventually runs up to or beyond the mentor's skill and perception, incompetent child becomes the highly competent adult—all a gift of the tutoring done by parent or friendly professional.

But stories do not always end well simply because they have happy beginnings or splendid moments of mutual respect and grace. What begins as a generous gift of trust may turn into a competing game or a vicious takeover attempt.

This is a chapter about roles and relationships. We must admit that we live and move in community. Indeed, each of us at any given moment sustains relationships in three or more significant systems. We have families, often two or more tribal groups to which we relate. We have the workplace with its interpersonal relationships and roles. And most of us sustain a set of social and fraternal ties through community, alma mater, or church. In all of these systems and more, we shift from one set of status role relationships to another. Since our life pilgrimage guarantees that we will live and move in these relationship systems, it is important to ask what impact our discipleship with Jesus has on those systems. But it is equally important for us to receive light for our roles from Jesus' teaching and His way of living out His values.

Each of us wrestles with issues of titles, respect, professional distance, and intimacy. Fallen social structures tend to follow a pattern by which roles determine relationships. Jesus offers us a pattern by which the relationship determines the role. In this Creation-Redemption model, the role is always a gift. In the painful fallen model with which we are much more familiar, roles are assigned, won, earned, or grasped forcibly.

Jesus gave us a clear word about roles, status, and relationships. When "the mother of the sons of Zebedee came to Jesus with her sons, bowing down, and making a request of

Him," Jesus took the occasion of this fallen expression of ambition to explain a very different doctrine about roles.

> Among the heathen, kings are tyrants and each minor official lords it over those beneath him. But among you it is quite different. Anyone wanting to be a leader among you must be your servant. And if you want to be right at the top, you must serve like a slave. Your attitude must be like My own, for I, the Messiah, did not come to be served, but to serve, and to give My life as a ransom for many. Matthew 20:25-28, TLB

There is likely no area of life which is so persistently in conflict with Jesus than is our lust for power—our self-centeredness. We need continually to look at ourselves, our goals, our ambitions, and let Jesus change us.

## IMAGE OF A SERVANT

The Christian doctrine of submission appears to be the apostles' equivalent teaching to Jesus' word on servanthood. Most often today the submission teaching seems largely but wrongly focused on efforts to define a woman's place in Christian teaching. It is common for pastors to call men to servanthood, and women to submission. But St. Paul uses submission as the directive to both men and women: "Submitting yourself to one another out of reverence for Christ: Wives . . . to your husbands. . . . Husbands . . . for your wives" (Ephesians 5).

In 1 Peter 3, Peter describes Jesus submitting to the abuse that led to His death, of slaves submitting to masters, of wives submitting to husbands, and of husbands, "in the same way" reverencing their wives, remembering that they are "joint-heirs of the promise" and that their prayers will not be answered if they do not so submit to their wives. And in the Peter passage, the submission in most cases is held up as the Christian alternative to retribution—to fighting back to get even with an adversary. But Paul offers mutual submission as a model which climaxes in images of head and body as one whole person, just as "two become one" in the doctrine of Creation. Hence, "submission to one another out of reverence for Christ" becomes the Creation-Redemption model of submission as a gift which husbands and wives present to each other for the synchrony of the new persona, the one-flesh person which is the marital unit.

We are not surprised, then, to find Jesus voluntarily demonstrating submission and servanthood in His intense teaching session during the last week of His life. Everything He has taught comes down to the week of "final exams." The most complete record of that week begins at John 13 and continues through the Resurrection. The fourth Gospel description of the Last Supper is put down in amazing detail.

> Jesus, knowing that the Father had given all things into His hands and that He had come from God, and was going back to God, rose from supper, and laid aside His garments; and took a towel and girded Himself. After that, He poured water into a basin and began to wash His disciples' feet, drying them with the towel that was wrapped around Him.
>
> John 13:3-5, KJV

Modern attempts at foot-washing as a sacrament or a re-enactment of that original liturgy are rarely successful. People scrub themselves before such a service, trim their toenails, and are determined to put their best foot forward. Most efforts turn out to be pale gestures toward the actual essence of the original foot-washing. There is every evidence that Jesus' washing of the feet was simply the minimum service offered to guests invited to a meal. The washing was necessary because the feet would have been stained from the unsanitary conditions of the streets as well as possibly bruised and cut from walking. Also, while eating, one's feet were positioned on a recliner couch just inches below the face of the next guest. Since the streets served as sewage disposal sites, offensive sores, odors and especially unsanitary flux collected from walking through the streets made foot-washing an important ritual.

Jesus, the host of a meal being served in a borrowed room, did what simply had to be done. The meaning of foot-washing as a Christian symbol came home to me early in my career with the backpacking course which we describe as "discipleship development through trail camping." I had cautioned the campers to pay attention to their feet. "If you suddenly become aware that you have feet, you can be sure that something is going wrong with them. Hot spots show up even before they are hot—simply as a mild discomfort. So stop, check the skin, apply an adhesive pad to the troubled spot, and you can avoid most blisters."

Four days into the week, Jeff came to me after the evening meal. I noticed that he was walking gingerly in open tennis shoes. "Mr. Joy, I think maybe you should look at my feet."

When I got his socks off, I saw a pair of badly blistered feet with reddening edges around the raw and broken sores. Add to this the fact that they hurt so bad that Jeff had passed up the occasional swim or playing under a waterfall we had indulged in, simply to avoid the pain of water on open blisters. His feet were dark with ground-in dirt. I sterilized my scissors, and with the alcohol bottle nearby, cleaned each broken blister and washed his feet in rubbing alcohol. The pain seemed worth it to Jeff, a tough and beautiful high school athlete who was embarrassed that his feet had literally gotten him down. When I had slipped clean white socks onto the now lightly bandaged feet, I knew he would be able to walk tomorrow.

It was the summer of 1979, with Jeff watching my work on his sore feet, that I saw the problem with modern "foot-washing services" I had participated in. I had spent nearly an hour with one pair of feet and the wounded pride of a young man.

## TRAINING OF SERVANTS

Jesus, wanting to establish a direct, purposeful experience on which to rest His teaching about servanthood, washed their feet. If you want to make a servant, be one. "Do you understand what I have done for You?" Jesus asked the disciples. Then He explained, so that no one could miss the point of His actions.

> "You call me Teacher and 'Lord,' and rightly so, for that is what I am. Now that I, your Lord and Teacher, have washed your feet, you also should wash one another's feet. I have set you an example that you should do as I have done for you. I tell you the truth, no servant is greater than his master, nor is a messenger greater than the one who sent him. Once you know these things, you will be blessed if you do them."                    John 13:12-17

"Show me how, and I think I can do it," is the plea of every eager learner. But it always seems easier to tell them than to show them. Jesus is indeed the Master Teacher. His demonstration set the stage for His demand that they be servants to one another.

I had the once-in-a-lifetime privilege of being with my daughter-in-law, Dorian, when the telephone connection to the Kosciusko County Hospital brought word that the doctors had given up working with her father who suffered a sudden and massive heart attack. Louis Luckenbill was gone. The Wilmore police had phoned me to say that an emergency call was waiting, but that Dorian's line was busy. I drove to the house to give her the 219 area number which certainly meant unexpected trouble. So I was there, but I was mostly helpless. There is no immediate or proper comfort for such loss. Yet, I was there.

Something happened to me in that hour or so as the loss registered with Dorian and she allowed me into the privacy of her fresh grief. Nearly five years later, and turning beyond mid-life and facing my own mortality, I suddenly realized that the episode had established a new level of trust. I later told Dorian, "When it comes time for me to die, I don't have any idea what the circumstances may be. But you are one of the people I am willing to have with me when I'm dying." And contemplating what death can involve, there are not many people I will want to see when I am moving toward that boundary.

So here we may have an unspoken hope embedded in Jesus' teaching. "I want you to wash each other's feet, and I am bound for circumstances in which I may be utterly and helplessly dependent on you to care for Me, when I am dying." They got their chance, but the lesson had not yet registered deeply enough for them to hang on.

Jesus addressed the realities of status and role. "You call Me Teacher and Lord, and you are right," is a plain statement of fact—their relationship made it clear that His responsibilities and theirs were different. Notice the titles that described the relationship. The titles did not give Jesus His authority, His wisdom, or His leadership. Instead, His leadership, wisdom, and authority necessitated title and status descriptions. This is radically different from modern and pagan systems which demand respect for persons according to their titles and role assignments. Respect should go to persons, not to offices or titles. Leadership is intrinsically a matter of a person's gifts and contributions. It is not something that happens when people announce themselves or are formally or legally designated as "leaders."

"No servant is greater than his master, nor is a messenger greater than the one who sent him." Do not miss the point here. Jesus has lowered Himself to the servant *task,* yet He is Teacher and Lord. It is as if He is saying, *You who use those titles of respect based on My service to you must get down here on the floor with Me to be servants—since there is nothing lower than a servant's task.* Indeed Jesus uses the same images to link them up with suffering and death.

> If the world hates you, keep in mind that it hated Me first. If you belonged to the world, it would love you as its own. As it is, you do not belong to the world, but I have chosen you out of the world. That is why the world hates you. Remember the words I spoke to you: "No servant is greater than his master." If they persecuted Me, they will persecute you also. If they obeyed My teaching, they will obey yours also. They will treat you this way because of My name, for they do not know the One who sent Me. If I had not come and spoken to them, they would not be guilty of sin. Now, however, they have no excuse for their sin. He who hates Me hates My Father as well. If I had not done among them what no one else did, they would not be guilty of sin. But now they have seen these miracles, and yet they have hated both Me and My Father. But this is to fulfill what is written in their Law: "they hated Me without reason." John 15:18-25

Far from suggesting that disciples or students will surpass the honor due to their teachers, Jesus flattens the competitive issue entirely—no learner is greater than his teacher.

We who live in the Ohio Valley tend to indulge in occasional seasonal idolatries. During baseball season we pay special attention to a regional hero named Pete Rose. In 1985, when Pete hit his 1,491st base hit and broke Ty Cobb's record, it wasn't only the scoreboard in Cincinnati that went crazy. Most of us did too. But a regional sportscaster got Pete Rose on camera and asked the question everyone thought they knew the answer to, "Does this mean that you are a greater ball player than Ty Cobb?"

"Nobody said anything about greater!" Pete exploded. "All it means is that I got one more base hit than Ty Cobb did!" And he went on to explain that if it had not been for Ty Cobb's phenomenal record of base hits, "I would have given up the game long ago. But his record stood out there in front of me as something that challenged me to stick with it. . . . Nobody said anything about greater!"

## CALLED TO GREATER THINGS

Most of us are ready to accept any idea that we may be better off than our forebears, even better looking or more gifted. But the idea that we might have more work to do or a greater assignment or even better resources, therefore an obligation to be greater in production, is one we have less interest in. It comes too close to the haunting warning of Jesus that "from everyone who has been given much, much will be demanded" (Luke 12:48). Magnified possibility carries with it an automatic magnified responsibility. And Jesus unfolded His teaching to put the stress on "doing greater things":

> Thomas said, "Lord, we don't know where You are going, so how can we know the way?"
>
> Jesus answered, "I am the way—and the truth and the life. No one comes to the Father ex-

cept through Me. If you really knew Me, you would know My Father as well. From now on, you do know Him and have seen Him. . . .

"Believe Me when I say that I am in the Father and the Father is in Me; or at least believe on the evidence of the miracles themselves. I tell you the truth, anyone who has faith in Me will do what I have been doing. He will do even greater things than these, because I am going to the Father. And I will do whatever you ask in My name, so that the Son may bring glory to the Father. You may ask Me for anything in My name, and I will do it."

John 14:5-14

What we discover is that doing greater things is not a measure of our independent resourcefulness. Instead, we are enabled to do greater things because we have Jesus' special and multiplied personal resources. He is now with the Father, in a cosmic and heavenly position. His unlimited resources are available for any concern or project we can imagine or identify— whatever we ask in His name.

"In His name." Whatever can this mean? It is at once the key to unlocking the resources for doing the same works as Jesus did and also for doing "greater works." Clearly, these are not magic words to sprinkle at the end of a prayer. But they do constitute a moral and spiritual filter through which we must pass with our motives and our works. If anything misses the spirit, the values, and the character of Jesus, it is none of His, and His resources simply are not available.

Many religious leaders seem eminently successful. Some even build empires through use of immoral and illegal means. "Success" in tangible, material terms often seduces us into believing, "They must be in the will of God because they achieve such results." But it takes only about five minutes of listening to the "fine print" to know that the filter of Jesus' character would expose these charlatans as clever magicians and evil people who seduce money and goods to feather their own luxury and to feed their lust for power.

Jesus is multiplied in the world today. My colleague, George Hunter, tells of a young woman from Sydney, Australia, who emigrated to the United States and made her way to Chicago. There she moved quickly into the fast lane, and within a few years was devastated. She prepared to take her life, but first phoned her father in Sydney to tell him of her suicide plan. He kept her on the phone for more than an hour, but without talking her out of killing herself.

When she hung up on him while he was continuing his case against her death, her father phoned a Methodist pastor in Sydney who had a reputation as a man of prayer. The pastor indicated that he would pray, but that he would also phone a pastor in Chicago. He got the pastor of Chicago Temple on the phone within moments of hanging up from the distraught father. The Chicago Temple pastor consulted a parish map and indicated that three of their members lived within two blocks of the woman's address. So, twenty minutes after she had hung up on her father in Sydney, one of the Methodist families along with police broke down the door so the emergency crew could evacuate her.

Today, the woman is a member of Chicago Temple. Dr. Hunter met her and asked, "How does it feel to be a member of this great church?"

"Oh, I don't think other people see what I do when I come to church. I see a church that is literally connected around the world. I know. I wouldn't be a Christian, and I wouldn't be alive if it weren't for this church."

When Dr. Hunter told the story recently during World Methodist Week, he connected it to the Pete Rose phenomenon of the ultimate base hit. "Nobody said we would be greater, but that we'd better be making more hits."

Exactly. Jesus is our "down link" from the resources of the Father and of all of heaven. But He is also our source of imagination and creativity, and by that divine energy we stand in an age of miraculous communications possibilities. Jesus was limited to the geography of Palestine, with one side trip into Egypt. He never used a telephone, a television camera, or a radio. Something would be terribly wrong if we weren't making "more hits." But the crux of the difference comes in another issue. Did Jesus succeed in transferring authority to the disciples? And if He did make the transfer, how did He do it and with what risks?

## "I CALL YOU FRIENDS"

If Jesus' servanthood teaching and His entire mission was to succeed, it would be evident by one thing—that His disciples obeyed Him. The evidence of that obedience was sufficiently on line before the crucifixion that Jesus described how their role and status had already changed. And He described the basis of their "promotion." They had been His servants, He had been their Teacher and Lord. Now, He had something very different in mind.

> "If you remain in Me and My words remain in you, ask whatever you wish, and it will be given you. This is to My Father's glory, that you bear much fruit, showing yourselves to be My disciples.
>
> "As the Father has loved Me, so have I loved you. Now remain in My love. If you obey My commands, you will remain in My love, just as I have obeyed My Father's commands and remain in His love. I have told you this so that My joy may be in you and that your joy may be complete. My command is this:

Love each other as I have loved you. No one has
greater love than the one who lays down his life for
his friends. You are My friends if you do what I
command. I no longer call you servants, because a
servant does not know his master's business. Instead,
I have called you friends, for everything that I
learned from My Father I have made known to you.
You did not choose Me, but I chose you to go and
bear fruit—fruit that will last. Then the Father will
give you whatever you ask in My name. This is My
command: Love each other."

John 15:7-20

Since Jesus was about to be removed from the corporate
structure of the first Christian movement, we might ask whether
these co-regents and joint-heirs of the kingdom of God were
ready. Was it too much teaching too fast?

If you trace Jesus' teaching from John 13 to 17, you see
that the teaching about the Holy Spirit is introduced in John
14, amplified in 15, and the doctrinal implications are unpacked
in John 16. Then, suddenly Jesus' prayer in John 17, which
makes no mention of the Holy Spirit.

Instead, Jesus seems to zero in on these human disciples
He has been teaching, and through them, by faith, reaches
down to all of us who were yet to believe on Jesus through their
message.

"Father . . . You have granted [Your Son] authority
over all men that He might give eternal life to all
those You have given Him. Now this is eternal life:
that they may know You, the only true God, and
Jesus Christ, whom You have sent. . . .

"Holy Father, protect them by the power of Your
name—the name You gave Me—so that they may be

> one as We are one. While I was with them, I pro-
> tected them and kept them safe by that name You
> gave Me. . . . Sanctify them by the truth; Your word
> is truth. As You sent Me into the world, I have sent
> them into the world.
>
> "My prayer is not for them alone. I pray also for
> those who will believe in Me through their message,
> that all of them may be one, Father, just as You are
> in Me and I am in You. May they also be in Us so
> that the world may believe that You have sent
> Me. . . ."                                    John 17

The absence of the Holy Spirit in the prayer reminds us
that Pentecost had not yet inaugurated that event by which God
plants Himself in humans by "purifying their hearts by faith."
But the powerful prayer here lifts the human participants to a
level of intimate participation in the purposes of God which is
unparalleled in history. Even Eden saw humans only "walking
with God in the cool of the day." Here Jesus lifts us up to an
intimacy and uses the language of marital union to paint a picture of "full knowing" of the business of God the Father and God
the Son: "Make them one, as You Father are in Me, and I in
You, let them be made one in Us, that the world may know and
believe."

## WHAT A CHURCH!

It is easy to ask whether the world has ever seen a true community of servants. We are so entangled in the worldly, fallen
models of status, rank, and power that in our best efforts we
damage each other through our greed, our competition, our
throwing around titles, ranks, and degrees of importance. But
Jesus clearly calls us to a role of servanthood, friendship, and
absolute mutual care and respect.

Dr. Ed Beck told our students of his occasional stops at the Olympic Training Center in Colorado Springs. Dr. Beck is a pastor there of a great church and makes hospital visits near the Center. "I enjoy watching these young aspiring athletes as they train," he said. On one occasion he discovered that the OTC was hosting a Special Olympics. He had arrived in time for only the final event—a sixty-yard dash by these young athletes whose worldwide motto is, "There are no losers—only winners."

Thirteen children lined up with considerable difficulty. They included several obvious Down's Syndrome children— those beautiful innocents Morris West has dubbed "the clowns of God." There were others with severely handicapping conditions, including some whose general coordination made it almost impossible to arrange at a starting line. Finally there was the crack of the starting gun. The children started moving, as if in slow motion. A few quickly took the lead.

Down the field about twenty yards, a young boy in the middle of the straggling pack fell slowly, and his cry started to rise even before his hands and face could have touched the cinders. And as the wail mounted higher, Dr. Beck reported how astonished he was. "I could not believe what was happening! The other twelve all came to a slow-motion stop. Those in front paused, turning, looking back over their shoulders; then moving full circle, they loped back to where the wailing young man lay. Those behind him continued toward him. The few who were near him were already stooping over him and bobbing up and down as if they were giant birds examining an unusual discovery.

"Within a couple of minutes all twelve were circled around the boy. We could no longer see him from the bleachers.

"Then two or three of the bobbing mass began to speak to the boy. 'Can—you—get—up?' they asked. There was no answer for a while. Then we heard it.

146

" 'I—can—get—up.' The tones were measured but sure.

"Then, his injuries became apparent to the other children. One little girl knelt down and with her cheek began to stroke his bleeding knee, as if to say, 'I give you healthy skin from my cheek for your broken skin on your knee.' I was amazed at this direct contact therapy. But a little boy seeing his bleeding elbow, lifted the arm so gently and kissed the elbow right on the bleeding and cinder-burned spot. Several of the children simply touched him.

"But in front of the injured young man a little girl smiled right up into his face. 'Are—you—ready?' she asked him repeatedly, bouncing as she spoke. And in a moment, it sounded as if all of the other twelve were asking the same thing, 'Are—you—ready? Are—you—ready?'

" 'I'm—ready!' he finally mustered, confidently, and inhaling to extend his height.

"Then I saw a sight I was not prepared for, as two of the children linked arms with the injured boy. Then one by one, the entire line of thirteen children linked up. To my utter amazement, they all started toward the finish line together."

They must have a set a new record for the longest sixty-yard dash in history. But Dr. Ed Beck, that sensitive pastor, exclaimed, "I hope I never forget that picture. That is what the church is supposed to be. Our motto, like the Special Olympics, needs to be, "There Are No Losers—Only Winners."

# WHO?

Among the heathen, kings are tyrants and each
minor official lords it over those beneath him.
But among you it is quite different. Anyone
wanting to be a leader among you must be your
servant.                              Matthew 20:25-26, TLB

## WHERE?

On a piece of paper, make a circle for each of your personal
systems, overlapping where they connect. In each circle make
an X for each significant contact person; write a word to denote
your role or status.

## WHAT?

Write one of the following words in each system, indicating
what is most important to you in each system: status, title, role,
power, respect received.

## WHY?

If relationships based on absolute mutual respect and unconditional positive regard were present in each of your systems, how
would each system be changed?

## WHEN?

Draw a box around the system which is most locked into the
fallen power model where competition, status, and control are
holding the people hostage. Circle in a bright color the system
most like Jesus: where servanthood and submission enrich relationships. Those systems are an important curriculum for your
faith.

# TEN

## CONFRONTING AND RELEASING

Bruce was last to join the circle of hikers. We were loaded down with our gear for a day's walk. Overnight we had put up our tarps in the Civil War battlefield north of Livingston. Today we would head north toward S-Tree, a high ridge with a fire tower overlooking Kentucky's central section of Daniel Boone National Forest.

"Do you have anything to say to the group?" I asked, when he finally got himself together and joined us. The night before, Bruce was mysteriously absent after the evening variety show and vespers. I had announced before closing prayer, "A few of you know that we had a painful episode today. So I want everyone else to know what happened. One of our campers hustled money from about five others younger than himself after he contacted a hitchhiker who had some pot. Then, when we arrived here at our campsite, the six of them smoked it. For at least four of them, it was a first experience. We still don't know the long-term effects of marijuana use, but among the people I know who use it, there is a consistent struggle with depression. So you can imagine that if any of these four young people ten years from now are giving up on whether life is worthwhile, it will be very hard on me, since I am responsible for them on this trip.

"The four campers I referred to have each voluntarily reported to me what happened. I am quite sure they are finished with marijuana. But let me suggest that if you are carrying some guilt that you need to get rid of, you can share it during Tarp Talk tonight. When the Bible speaks of repentance, it is talking about 'coming home to the truth.' " I prayed and sent them off in their trail families.

Bruce had not been with us for that trail family conversation. He was, however, in his sleeping bag when we awakened the next morning. Now, he and I faced one another in our trail family circle.

"I'm not going to say anything! You don't have anything on me!" Bruce was present now, but he was frozen up with rage or fear—or both.

"Remember, Bruce, that I told everybody as we left the seminary parking lot that there was nothing that could happen on the trip that would cause us to send anyone home. That still holds. I have respected you from the moment I met you. The first day, the two of us hung together on our buddy system— you helping me with my pack; I helped you get into yours after every break. We walked and talked together most of the day. And I liked what I learned about you. But now I know something that troubles me a lot and you aren't willing to talk about it. Bruce, you are a dangerous person. You are dangerous to yourself, and you are dangerous to other people. For the rest of the week, you are 'grounded.' I am asking you never to be out of my sight.

"Now look at me," I said, as the eight of us were standing in a tight circle, arms around the shoulders ready for our morning prayer before we hit the trail. "I am releasing you to Satan, but I am doing it because you have chosen to live deceptively. I want you to know that I know that none of us can control you or keep you from following the choices you have made. So you are free to go ahead and do it your way. But I pray that you will soon hit the end of the rope and will be ready to come home to the truth." Then we huddled in and prayed and started our fifteen miles of hiking for the day.

Most of us yearn for days without pain, without conflict, and without contact with trouble, evil, or the junk that clutters so much of the human experience landscape. But the test of our faith, remember, comes in the crucibles of life. And life in any culture today, is going to bring us almost daily brushes with unpleasantness and trouble. What do you say to moral failure in close associates? Well, of course, you can buy into the awful privatism of our times, the theory that claims everybody is entitled to go to hell in their own way. But such an attitude really means that hell is already begun, and you are planted in its middle.

In this final chapter, we tackle the toughest responsibility that comes with the territory of living in obedience to Jesus. What do we say to sin and moral failure? Since we cannot ignore it, we need abundant help in meeting corruption in our environment, in ways that are profoundly Christian.

There is an amazing "final teaching" from Jesus following the Resurrection. Here it is. From it we will have to decide what our options are, in terms of our responsibility about the sins of others.

> On the evening of that first day of the week, when the disciples were together, with the doors locked for fear of the Jews, Jesus came and stood among them and said, "Peace be with you!" After He had said this, He showed them His hands and side. The disciples were overjoyed when they saw the Lord.
> Again Jesus said, "Peace be with you! As the Father has sent Me, I am sending you." And with that He breathed on them and said, "Receive the Holy Spirit. If you forgive anyone his sins, they are forgiven. If you do not forgive them, they are not forgiven."  John 20:19-23

## FEAR AND SHALOM

The first response to trouble is usually raw fear. We are afraid because we sense a risk to life and safety. Such fear is "standard equipment on all models," and when the hair follicles go perpendicular on the back of your neck at the sight of a snake, you are sensing this "primal fear."

A strange thing happens when fear strikes. The higher brain, consisting of its well-known two hemispheres, literally becomes impaired and virtually shuts down. In that part of the brain are our powers of speech and of logical reasoning. Leslie A. Hart[1] refers to this fear-triggered shut down as "down shifting." The core of the brain which governs basic body functions still operates, including the center for controlling basic juices, including the production of adrenaline. Adrenaline pumps into the bloodstream and speeds up the heart and respiration to get more oxygen to the brain and the muscles. It raises the hair follicles, and sets up the ability to fight or to run. But you are not yourself rationally. You are the victim of your juices. Most of us have found ourselves helpless in the face of a traffic emergency and have beaten on the dashboard or simply have screamed—unable to report to the driver in any coherent way what was really happening. Airliners crash and a few survivors report that although the crash was visibly imminent, nobody was saying anything as the plane went down. Speech was paralyzed in those final moments.

Fear is debilitating. Since it turns toward primal preservation, it jumps to wrong conclusions. Sometimes the wrong conclusions are about the source of the fear itself. Watch fear work on the disciples after the Resurrection.

"On the evening of that first day of the week, when the disciples were together, with the doors locked for fear of the Jews. . . ." They have locked the doors. Jesus has been executed. What more convincing signal do they need. If the dominoes begin to fall, surely they are quickly in line to be wiped out next. The Jews have found a means of bypassing civil authority and killing off whomever they will. So the fear focus is on the group that wields the death sentence.

In our world, there are deadly forces named AIDS, terrorism, and, from time to time, national and ethnic groups. Those are the big visible enemies. But ask any parent and you learn that there are other fears which rob their nights of sleep. How do you launch a child in such a troubled world? How do you nurture honesty and decency and protect against experimentation and promiscuity among the young?

Ask any young person, and you get a sense that doomsday may be nearer than you thought. "Will I be allowed to grow up, have a career, marry, and bring children into the world, or will my future go up in a nuclear blast or perish in a nuclear winter?" All of us deal with fears which rob us of our best responses. Indeed, in our paralyzed speechlessness, we are often victims who contribute to the fulfillment of our own prophecies of doom.

## THE GIFT OF SHALOM!

Jesus came and stood among them and said, "Peace be unto you!" After He had said this, He showed them His hands and side. The disciples were overjoyed when they saw the Lord.

Again Jesus said, "Peace be with you!"

The cure for fear is peace! *Shalom* is much larger than our word for peace. It denotes total well-being. It is the ideal greeting or parting word. It falls easily from the lips whenever we want to express the idea, "So long as we have each other, nothing can destroy us."

But the greater cure for their fear was Jesus Himself! Jesus walking in on these paralyzed, frightened believers was solid proof that the fear was pointless, because death—the primal enemy—is powerless.

So if we need to get our voices back, be able to reason straight again, and turn our sleepless nights into restful slumber, we too need for Jesus to appear and to defuse our fears.

## UNLIKELY MISSION

"As the Father has sent Me, I am sending you." If we could capture the actual picture, it would look like a comic strip. Here are the eleven disciples paralyzed, fear nibbling like piranahs at their stomachs. If they ever heard or knew any words of hope or comfort or healing, they have now forgotten them. They pace their private, self-imposed dungeon, as if it were locked from outside and not inside. They are, to put it in our idiom, a mess! Then, in a matter of a few seconds, it appears, they get their senses back and they are exuberant! "They were overjoyed when they saw the Lord."

And then Jesus does the most improbable thing anyone has ever done on this planet. He looks into the faces of that fear-decimated group of men and announces that the incarnation is still on. Just as the Father sent Jesus in human flesh and blood, so also Jesus is sending the eleven disciples in flesh that has recently quivered with fear, run from encounter with evil, and has even abandoned Jesus, one of them to the point of actual denial.

And with that Jesus breathed on them and said, "Receive the Holy Spirit."

God knew they needed new breath. The stench of denial and abandonment simmered for seventy-two hours over a mounting flame of fear for their lives. Fear had brought them to the brink of abandoning all of the visions of their futures, and had stunk up the air of life for them.

In the Creation, God "breathed into Adam the breath of life" and the first human became a "thing alive." This *nephesh* gift, shared among all of the creatures of the sixth day, denoted aliveness, and the vitality of throbbing warm-bloodedness. It was likely equated with "soulishness" or pure animal vitality. This soulishness in humans seems always vulnerable to the seduction of pure pleasure. The rich fool complained, "What shall I do? . . . I will tear down my barns and build greater! . . . And I will say to my soul, 'Soul, thou hast much goods laid up for many years; take thine ease, eat drink, and be merry.' But God said unto him, 'Thou fool, this night thy soul shall be required of thee. . .' "

Jesus is not breathing *nephesh* or animal spirit into these men. The first Adam was made a "thing alive," but Jesus makes us "temples of the Spirit of God." The breath Jesus breathes on them is quite different, though the imagery reminds us of Genesis.

The breath of Genesis suggests that it was linked with respiration—literally pumping up Adam to release the first human being as living and breathing, literally "a thing alive." But here the men are technically alive, living and breathing. So Jesus breathing on them lacks the intimate mouth-to-mouth resuscitation imagery which is evoked by Genesis 2.

Not long ago, I asked a question of a congregation. "What do you think it looked like when Jesus breathed on them?" Then I offered a regret that the Russians missed the Los Angeles Olympics. "I missed their victory celebrations, so strange to Westerners. Those exuberant athletes from the east have preserved for us what St. Paul evidently referred to as 'the holy kiss.' Russian athletes embracing, kissing each cheek in turn," I suggested, "may have illustrated for us how Jesus 'breathed on them,' as He embraced them one by one."

A Turkish student at nearby Texas Tech University was in the congregation and greeted me afterward. He said, "I think I know what Jesus was doing when He 'breathed on them.' In my country, the senior member of the family is the last to enter the room on any festive family occasion. And when the patriarch enters, all become very quiet. Looking around at everyone, our revered leader will take quick and deep breaths, holding the air inside. Then, moving quickly around all of us who have gathered into a circle, he slowly releases his breath in our direction. He does not stop and he does not take another fresh breath. We all receive the same breath on us. When we are breathing his own breath, we are part of him and he has transmitted himself to the coming generations. I think this is what the passage is describing."

We anticipate Pentecost, of course, when we hear Jesus' words about the Holy Spirit. But the image of "the breath of Jesus" carrying the Holy Spirit into the energy centers of the eleven apostles is at once more intimate than the account by Luke in Acts, which describes that mass meeting outpouring of the Holy Spirit as being accompanied by "the sound of a mighty rushing [breath] wind." Both pictures make clear the inner driving force of Jesus within to motivate, purify, and equip Christians. Receiving the Holy Spirit is linked forever to Jesus' breath, and to the mission of Jesus continued through the apostles and all who believe on Jesus through their words.

## DO JESUS' WORK: FORGIVENESS

We are planted in a moral universe where failure, shipwreck, and agony are daily realities. Much of Jesus' energy seems to have been invested in the healing and restoration of victims of evil. It will be no different for us. Any day's work will bring us in contact with people suffering, bent down beneath the load of shame, humiliation, guilt, and blame. Jesus tells us what to do— "If you forgive anyone his sins, they are forgiven. . . ."

It would be easier if Jesus had told us to send people to the preacher, the priest, or the rabbi where "absolution" and rituals of restitution and forgiveness are brokered. The word is painfully clear—we are to "forgive sins," and when we do "they are forgiven."

Living, as we do, in a world where we can hardly keep up with forgiving and being forgiven for our stupidity and our carelessness in interpersonal relationships, it seems fatuous to imagine that *we* are to "forgive other people's sins." We say, "Of course, I can forgive people if they have hurt me or sinned against me." But that is hardly what Jesus was talking about.

Jesus was leaving this planet. He was leaving behind a frightened, failing group of people, and He was putting His work in their hands. They would have these resources to back them up:

† Jesus, Himself, promised to empower them and to answer their prayers.

† Jesus made the bold statement that they would do greater works then He did.

† He assured the apostles that they would have all of His power which He received from the Father: "As the Father has sent Me, so send I you."

† Now, Jesus, breathing on them charged them with the power of the Holy Spirit.

With this lineup of resources, Jesus presents a gift to a troubled world. "There is still hope for you," is the message. "There is healing, restoration, and new life. Just as God has created humanity 'very good,' so also people can be made new through the forgiveness of their sins. Shame and guilt are no longer life sentences. Find a believer on whom the Holy Spirit has been breathed, and you can be set free from sin—from whatever is destroying you!"

Every fall I draft a final exam for a course in human development and ministry. I always construct a case study and ask the students to generate a conversation with a troubled person who has voluntarily confessed having lost control and indulged in destructive, sinful behavior. A consistent pattern shows up each season. It goes like this in a typical scenario: "I would thank the person for telling me everything, and then I would urge them to confess to God in order to be forgiven." I affirm the good pastoral instincts. But John 20:23 has simply not registered with us. So, I often write in the margin, "Why do you think they have voluntarily unloaded everything to you. *You* are the one to pronounce their forgiveness."

But humans forgiving sins? The Jews considered such a thing blasphemy. But Jesus insists. Likely the incarnation of God in Jesus bridged the gap between the sovereign and holy God and the earthbound fallen human race so effectively that Jesus determined to continue the incarnation—in ministry "in Jesus' name." Traditional folk like ourselves are still likely to cringe or even cry out "Blasphemy!" when someone calls us to such a radical obedience. But the world waits to discover that forgiveness is as close as a believing, Spirit-breathed neighbor. Many of the troubled people seem to be well ahead of us: they seem to know that we have the power to forgive sins. Listen to the talk shows, and read the mail of any minor Christian celebrity. Hurting people are eager to tell all. The only condition seems to be their sense that they can trust the listener or reader of their confessions. But timid, faltering witnesses that we are, most often we withdraw or try to deflect the confession directly to God. It is easy to wonder whether, indeed, we have ever allowed Jesus to breathe on us or whether the commission is ours for our time.

Sometimes this continuing incarnational "absolution" is nonverbal. And sometimes the confession never finds words. During my late teen years, Eugene Layson was my secret admired mentor. I wrestled with feelings of inferiority that occasionally dipped into shame with the accumulating sins of my youth. While I never sat down with Gene in a session I initiated simply to name my sins, Gene's knowledge of my failures opened an unspoken tunnel of trust between us. And he never wavered in his affirmation of me. He gave me the idea that I could go on in my walk with God, and that in going I would be healed. But neither Gene nor I ever named the confession or the absolution. Yet I knew that if Gene Layson, respected and godly man, could affirm me in every way, then God surely could accept me too. Forgiveness is literally at the human level first; the believer is given authority to speak for God.

Only this week I spent six hours, nonstop, with Dale, whom I met eighteen months ago on a thin wedge of good providence. Lecturing at Forest Home for a couples' retreat, I named five Los Angeles acquaintances from 1939—beautiful teen delegates to the Free Methodist General Conference of Youth. They had been weekend guests at my rural church in Kansas. "Someone here must have known these folks," I said, listing five names I had memorized at the age of eleven. "And I am eager to know what may have happened to them, if any of you know."

As that first evening wound down, I learned the stories of all five of my admired quintet from so long ago. And not at all to my surprise, I discovered that some of the family members were in the retreat. A grandson of one of the young women from 1939 was said to be registered for a young adult retreat at the same conference center, but in another location. It was Dale. So as we were lined up to grab our transportation back down to Los Angeles, someone pointed him out about to load onto a church bus. I walked up to him.

"I knew your grandmother as a young beautiful woman in 1939," I began, introducing myself.

He was startled, of course, but when he heard my name, he countered, "I almost broke away from my retreat to come over to see you, Dr. Joy. When I heard that you were talking about bonding and the image of God and all of that, I wanted to hear what you had to say. My girlfriend of three years broke up with me last month, and I'm almost out of my mind."

I listened for less than five minutes and the bus was rolling out, so I gave him my personal card and the quick advice, "Whatever you do, take time to grieve. Don't let anybody talk you into trying to date again until you have had time to reflect and to let Jesus turn your losses into the pure gold that comes with healing of your grief. And write to me if you think it would help."

More than a year passed. I wondered about Dale but did not worry. Now, a month ago I had a letter from Dale.

"I have not been able to deal with my problems well or to let God really work in my life either. Life is becoming very stressful. I feel I need therapy from a psychological standpoint and probably mental, too. I am afraid because I have a hard time trusting anyone, and though I know that God is there, I am unable to seek His help. I lack the wisdom. I know I am not well. My emotions are bringing on psychosomatic illnesses too, I'm afraid. I suffer from migraine headaches, for example. Since speaking with you for a few minutes at Forest Home, I feel I can trust you and that maybe you will be able to help me."

As I read the letter two or three times, I decided to put a local emergency contact person's name and phone number in his hands. I worried that the letter might be a very overripe cry for help. I picked up the phone to try also to make voice contact, and was able to give Dale Los Angeles dates only five weeks away, where we could be together. We had dinner at Knott's Berry Farm and were still there six hours later. The broken relationship had, indeed, left Dale devastated. This devastation in young men is very widespread, it turns out, contrary to the popular folklore. Dale thought I had seen right through him at Forest Home.

"I told you that we were sexual from December until June, didn't I?"

"No. But I knew you were deeply bonded to Kerri."

"Right after it happened, I told my pastor everything. He took me through the Scriptures to show me that I needed to confess my sexual sins. And he insisted that I was not really supposed to feel attached to her since we were not joined together in the sight of God. It didn't help much, but I tried to pray the repentance prayer he asked me to pray. I haven't been back to church since we talked. I feel like God is very far away. And I feel like such a failure. I'm ashamed to go around the church anymore."

"Let me tell you that you are wonderfully made and the bond was a profound one. 'What God joins together' refers to the universal bond that always works when two basically honest people become intimate. No wonder you are feeling abandoned. You are suffering all of the effects of a divorce. You are spared the legal hassles, likely, but your young sense of trust and integrity have been badly bruised. And to be rejected as you were would leave any healthy person devastated. So I am going to join you in your grief.

"Now look at me," I said. "On the authority of the words of Jesus in John 20:23, I want to tell you that your sins are forgiven. Since you named them here just now, I want you to let them go. Let me have them. Jesus wants you to be absolutely free of guilt. You can trust again. And I can assure you that God treasures you and grieves with you."

We began to pray at 10:45, easily and spontaneously. Dale spent nearly fifteen minutes in celebrating God's goodness and faithfulness to him through all of his agony and pain. By the time he crawled into his car to drive across the basin to his suburb, Dale was free of shame and guilt and quite aware, again, of the rising energy that comes from an intimate walk with God.

I caution my students that if they fumble the ball, when someone tests them with a deep and painful story which exposes feelings of guilt and shame, that they may be fulfilling Jesus' final charge—by terrifying default! They may be retaining sin instead of forgiving it. In their good intentions of calling for a clean confession somewhere else, to some other person, they have trivialized what the sinner knows to be the only route to forgiveness that works: they need to see the forgiveness in flesh and blood before their very eyes—incarnated in Holy Spirit-empowered words of absolution.

## *DO JESUS' WORK: BIND PEOPLE TO TRUTH!*

*"If you do not forgive them, they are not forgiven."* There it is. Jesus is as awesome in stating the negative pole of unforgiveness as He was in demanding that we pronounce forgiveness. We may as well face it—if any human being withholds forgiveness to the one who cries out to be forgiven, he has locked the victim into a prison cell of sin. It makes little difference whether the guilt was directly in proportion to a real failure or whether it was simply shame or feelings of humiliation. The withholding of forgiveness turns it into absolutely destructive reality.

It was noted theologian Mildred Wynkoop[2] who first opened up the John 20 passages in these radical terms for me. And as she did so in Royal Auditorium during a lectureship at Asbury Seminary, she told of a young woman, the last passenger in a car pool, who found herself being taken into a gigantic city park where the driver forcibly raped her. She was so humiliated she told no one, but in a few months realized that she must be pregnant and saw a physician. Only then did she open the subject separately with two women at her church. Each turned the conversation in the same way.

"What did you do to provoke him to rape you?"

"Today," Dr. Wynkoop reported, "the young woman still commutes each day to work. She puts a five-year-old son in day care each morning and picks him up each evening. She is almost never in church. Two women 'made to be sin what was no sin' for that young woman. 'If you do not forgive them, they are not forgiven.' "

I began this chapter with the story of Bruce. I call the encounter with Bruce an example of "binding people to the truth." At the time, I had no idea that Bruce had been expelled from two high schools. He was unable to live at home, and was currently being passed around to relatives; the backpacking trip was an easy week for the host family.

Jesus' command to deal with rebellious sin makes us uncomfortable, if we want to live perpetually in pleasantness. But Jesus' command to retain the sins of people who must be bound to the truth of their own responsibility rings true with the cryptic words in Hebrews 12:5.5: "The Lord disciplines those whom He loves, and He punishes everyone He accepts as a son." St. Paul's sword-like imagery in 1 Corinthians 5:4-5 pushes the idea of confrontation even further: "When you are assembled in the name of our Lord Jesus and I am with you in spirit, and the power of our Lord Jesus is present, hand this man over to Satan, so that his sinful nature may be destroyed and his spirit saved on the day of the Lord." Paul writes a more final sounding word of separation in 1 Timothy 1:19-20: "Some have rejected [faith and a good conscience] and so have shipwrecked their faith. Among them are Hymenaeus and Alexander, whom I have handed over to Satan to be taught not to blaspheme."

As we broke out of our prayer huddle, Bruce quickly walked out ahead to be alone and away from us. None of us could know what he was thinking. But Chris, a young man recently out of the drug culture, asked if he could walk with Bruce and we urged him ahead. Two hours later Chris returned to say that Bruce wanted to talk. The eight of us extended the break through the lunch hour as Bruce unfolded an almost complete biography of destructive behavior laced among abusive and violent family patterns across his lifetime. We were cemented in a closing liturgy of prayer and healing.

In our pilgrimage of faith, we come squarely up against the fact that we are responsible for dealing with pain, failure, and sin in other people's lives. We have been charged with responsibility both to confront the brazen and rebellious, and to freely tap God's resources in Jesus to announce boldly that sins of the penitent are forgiven. We don't have the luxury of "referring" the penitent to clergy or professional evangelists. We are Jesus' "incarnational saviours," and our life pain accumulated and transformed is our membership card in the specially gifted cadre of ministers of healing and reconciliation.

# Who?

As the Father has sent Me, I am sending you.

John 20:21

## WHERE?

Look at those systems circles you drew for chapter 9. Put names by the people symbols in the circles. Now box in each of those you know to be struggling with some painful failure or pattern of destruction.

## WHAT?

Put a double box around those who have voluntarily opened up their failure or pain to you. If your response carried a message of forgiveness or shared carrying of the burden, shoot out some sunlight shafts from the box of the person.

## WHY?

If being a Christian has as its chief motive getting free of pain and sin, then why would Jesus throw us back, head first, into other people's problems? Why, indeed!

## WHEN?

Put a mark by those people in your systems who are into destructive patterns, and are not voluntarily open with you. Will you let them destroy themselves and other people? Will you have to answer to Jesus for not confronting them? When will you make that call?

# SELECTED READINGS IN CHRISTIAN SPIRITUALITY

Let me suggest the following brief collection of books as tools for seeing life steadily and seeing it whole. Such a view of life easily translates into God's curriculum for spiritual formation. Most of them are easily available and provide engaging reading because of their urgent agendas placed in our present culture.

*Living in Relationships*

Robert Bellah, et al., *Habits of the Heart*
Donald Joy, *Bonding: Relationships in the Image of God*
Donald Joy, *Re-Bonding: Preventing and Restoring Damaged Relationships*
Donald and Robbie Joy, *Lovers: Whatever Happened to Eden?*
Donald Joy, *Parents, Kids, and Sexual Integrity*
Richard Foster, *Money, Sex, and Power*
Robert Mulholland, *Shaped by the Word*
Gary Smalley and John Trent, *The Blessing*
Jim Talley and Bobby Reid, *Too Close, Too Soon*
Walter Wangerin, *As for Me and My House*

*Life as Unfolding Development*

Paul W. Chilcote, *Wesley Speaks on Christian Vocation*
James W. Fowler, et al., *Trajectories*
James W. Fowler, *Becoming Adult, Becoming Christian*
James W. Fowler, *Faith Development and Pastoral Care*
James W. Fowler and Jim Keen, *Life Maps*
Belle Valerie Gaunt and George Trevelyan, *A Tent in Which to Pass a Summer's Night*
Donald Joy, ed., *Moral Development Foundations*
Daniel Levinson, et al., *The Seasons of a Man's Life*

Sharon Parks, *The Critical Years: The Young Adult Search for a Faith to Live By*

Catherine Stonehouse, *Patterns in Moral Development*

*Pain, Tragedy, and Transformation*

James Dobson, *Love Must Be Tough*

R.C. Sproul, *Stronger Than Steel: The Wayne Alderson Story*

Dag Hammarskjold, *Markings*

C.S. Lewis, *Pilgrim's Regress*

C.S. Lewis, *Surprised by Joy*

M. Scott Peck, *The Road Less Traveled*

M. Scott Peck, *People of the Lie*

M. Scott Peck, *Different Drum*

Walter Wangerin, *Orphean Passages*

Mildred Wynkoop, *A Theology of Love*

# FOR FURTHER READING

The following materials are suggested to help you increase your understanding of Spiritual Formation, and more importantly, to help you grow in your faith. Readings are categorized under basic headings having to do with our formation. Most of the books are in print at the time of this compilation. The few which are not can be obtained from most college and seminary libraries in your area. In addition to these resources, please use the footnotes as further means of exploring the various topics developed in this book.

*General Readings*
1. Leslie Weatherhead, *The Transforming Friendship*
2. Steve Harper, *Devotional Life in the Wesleyan Tradition*
3. Maxie Dunnam, *Alive in Christ*
4. E. Stanley Jones, *The Way*
5. Henri Nouwen, *Making All Things New*
6. Evelyn Underhill, *The Spiritual Life*
7. Alan Jones & Rachel Homer, *Living in the Spirit*
8. Iris Cully, *Education for Spiritual Growth*
9. Benedict Groeschel, *Spiritual Passages*

*Scripture*
1. Robert Mulholland, *Shaped by the Word*
2. David Thompson, *Bible Study That Works*
3. Susan Muto, *A Guide to Spiritual Reading*
4. Thomas Merton, *Opening the Bible*
5. H.A. Nielsen, *The Bible As If for the First Time*

*Prayer*
1. Harry E. Fosdick, *The Meaning of Prayer*
2. Dick Eastman, *The Hour That Changes the World*
3. Kenneth Leech, *True Prayer*
4. Anthony Bloom, *Beginning to Pray*
5. Maxie Dunnam, *The Workbook of Living Prayer*
6. O. Hallesby, *Prayer*

*The Lord's Supper*
1. William Willimon, *Sunday Dinner*
2. William Barclay, *The Lord's Supper*
3. Martin Marty, *The Lord's Supper*

*Fasting*
1. Richard Foster, *Celebration of Discipline* (helpful chapter)
2. Tilden Edwards, *Living Simply Through the Day* (helpful chapter)

*Direction/Accountability*
1. David Watson, *Accountable Discipleship*
2. Tilden Edwards, *Spiritual Friend*
3. Kenneth Leech, *Soul Friend*
4. Robert Coleman, *The Master Plan of Evangelism*

*Personality and Spiritual Development*
1. David Keirsey, *Please Understand Me*
2. Harold Grant, *From Image to Likeness*
3. Christopher Bryant, *The River Within*
4. Chester Michael, *Prayer and Temperament*

*The Holy Spirit*
1. Billy Graham, *The Holy Spirit*
2. Kenneth Kinghorn, *The Gifts of the Spirit*

3. Myron Augsburger, *Quench Not the Spirit*

*Discipline and Disciplines*
1. Richard Foster, *Celebration of Discipline*
2. Gordon MacDonald, *Ordering Your Private World*
3. Albert E. Day, *Discipline and Discovery*\*
4. James Earl Massey, *Spiritual Disciplines*
5. Maxie Dunnam, *The Workbook of Spiritual Disciplines*

*History of Christian Spirituality*
1. Urban Holmes, *A History of Christian Spirituality*
2. Alan Jones & Rachel Hosmer, *Living in the Spirit* (helpful chapter)

*Devotional Classics* (Introduction to)
1. Tilden Edwards, *The Living Testament: The Essential Writings Since the New Testament*
2. Thomas Kepler, *An Anthology of Devotional Literature*
3. *The Upper Room Devotional Classics*
4. Paulist Press Series, *The Classics of Western Spirituality*

*Social Spirituality*
1. John Carmody, *Holistic Spirituality*
2. William Stringfellow, *The Politics of Spirituality*
3. Dietrich Bonhoeffer, *Life Together*
4. Thomas Kelly, *A Testament of Devotion* (helpful chapter)
5. Henri Nouwen, *Gracias!*
6. Henri Nouwen, *Compassion*

*Ministry and Spiritual Formation*
1. Edward Bratcher, *The Walk on Water Syndrome*
2. Henri Nouwen, *The Living Reminder*
3. Louis McBirney, *Every Pastor Needs a Pastor*

4. Henri Nouwen, *Creative Ministry*
5. Oswald Sanders, *Spiritual Leadership*

*Devotional Guides and Prayer Books*
1. Rueben Job, *The Upper Room Guide to Prayer for Ministers and Other Servants*
2. Bob Benson, *Disciplines for the Inner Life*
3. John Baille, *A Diary of Private Prayer*
4. Charles Swindoll, *Growing Strong in the Seasons of Life*
5. John Doberstein, *The Minister's Prayer Book*
6. The Episcopalian *Book of Common Prayer*

# NOTES

## Chapter One

1. See the treatment of the structure and meaning of this passage in my *Bonding: Relationships in the Image of God*, chapter 1, "Who's Holding Your Trampoline?" (Waco, Texas: Word, Inc., 1985).

## Chapter Two

1. See my *Bonding: Relationships in the Image of God* (Waco, Texas: Word, Inc., 1985), for the details on birth bonding, including medical documentation.

## Chapter Three

1. Copyright, 1903, Lorenz Publishing Company, cited from Alfred B. Smith, *Favorites Number Two* (Grand Rapids, Zondervan Publishing, 1946).
2. See Jean Piaget, *The Moral Judgment of the Child* (Free Press, 1965).
3. See R.C. Sproul, *Stronger than Steel: the Wayne Alderson Story* (San Francisco: Harper and Row, Publishers, 1980).
4. Daniel Levinson, et al. *The Seasons of a Man's Life* (New York: Ballantine, 1978).
5. See "Who's Holding Your Trampoline?" in *Bonding: Relationships in the Image of God,* (Waco, Texas: Word, Inc., 1985).

# Chapter Four

1. Harry Harlow has become famous for his work with rhesus monkeys. In the audio-tape addresses entitled *Speaking of Love: Theory and Therapy* (New York: McGraw Hill, Educational Resources Associates, 1974), he describes the complex gestures of friendship he observes developmentally. Of the monkeys he says, "They have done more for me than I have done for them." Harlow describes the "peer love" gestures essential to their healthy development, noting that humans lack even a vocabulary to describe a similarly important phase of development in humans. It was his comment to which I listened more than ten years ago that has made me impatient with the fact that we neglect early pubescent friendship development in our young.

2. Dr. E. Mansell Pattison reports on his findings about the healthy "psychosocial kinship system" in his *Pastor and Parish—A Systems Approach* (Philadelphia: Fortress Press, 1977, pp. 18-19). In "Who's Holding Your Trampoline?" chapter 1 in my *Bonding: Relationships in the Image of God*, (Waco, Texas: Word, Inc., 1985), I unravel some of the implications for a healthy view of relationships.

3. Dr. James Fowler made this statement in an address at the National Association of Professors of Christian Education in Danvers, Massachusetts, Friday morning, October 23, 1987. His Christian perspective is best expressed in *Becoming Adult, Becoming Christian* (San Francisco: Harper and Row Publishers).

4. See Erik Erikson, *Childhood and Society* (New York: W.W. Norton), especially chapter 7, "The Eight Ages of Man."

5. See "Pair Bonding: What God Joins Together," chapter 3 in my *Bonding: Relationships in the Image of God* (Waco, Texas: Word, Inc., 1985), for additional help in discriminating between the glue of God and conventional marriage.

6. See Matthew 19:12, where Jesus makes clear the sacrifice required to covenant Christian celibacy and service.

# Chapter Five

1. C.S. Lewis, *The Great Divorce* (New York: Macmillan, 1946) p. 72.
2. Dag Hammerskjold, *Markings* (New York: Alfred A. Knopf, 1964) p. 15.
3. See my discussion of the secular trend in chapter 3, "The Adolescent Crucible: All Dressed Up with No Place to Go!" in *Parents, Kids, and Sexual Integrity* (Waco, Texas: Word, Inc., 1988).
4. Patrick Carnes, *Out of the Shadows: Understanding Sexual Addiction* (Minneapolis: CompCare Press).
5. E. Mansell Pattison, " 'Ex-Gays' " Religiously Mediated Change in Homosexuals" in *The American Journal of Psychiatry*, (vol. 137:12, 1980) 1553-1562.
6. See my *Re-Bonding: Preventing and Restoring Damaged Relationships* for an extensive treatment of fornication, adultery, divorce, and patterns of recovery from sexual trouble, damage, and addiction.
7. See "Who's Holding My Trampoline?" in my *Bonding: Relationships in the Image of God*, to examine the absolute necessity of continuing support from a cluster of people in order to maintain a healthy and spiritually sound perspective.

# Chapter Six

1. Paul Wesley Chilcote, *Wesley Speaks on Christian Vocation* (Nashville: Discipleship Resources, 1987) p. vii.
2. Marlene Mayr, *Modern Masters of Religious Education* (Birmingham: Religious Education Press, 1983) pp. 188-196.
3. One of the most straightforward current versions of the idea that male and female "functions" must dictate roles, with primitive cultural sexism laced throughout, is found in Weldon M.

Hardenbrook's *Missing from Action* (New York: Thomas Nelson, 1987). His discussion of the problem with males in America today revolves almost entirely in their loss of "male function" as "head of the house." "Why are some people so offended at the idea of male headship that they would call for the abolition of marriage? I am convinced it is due to a gross misunderstanding of the concept of headship, a confusion between a person's value and a person's function" (p. 145). Instead of seeing the male-female relationship as one of wholeness, "two becoming one flesh," or of unity—"head and body as forming a unity: Christ and church; husband and body," he violates the one-person metaphor and places the husband in "headship" clearly denoting a violent, hierarchical, corporate executive version.

See our *Lovers: Whatever Happened to Eden?* for a wholistic opening of the biblical material stressing relationship, not function, as the key to a healthy male and female development and continuing vitality. A "functional" view of persons denotes the ultimate triumph of Satan. In Genesis 3, the male renames Isshah, his mirror image, and calls her by a functional name: "Eve: baby maker." This opens the door to polygamy and prostitution and the historical abuses of women as property, as mere functional objects. Today, abortion, euthanasia, and suicide are clear inheritances of our "functionalism," by which any person may determine the "utilitarian" value of a person and may then terminate life when it ceases to have functional value.

In a "functional view of marriage," recommended throughout Hardenbrook's *Missing from Action*, any impairment in the physical endowment of either husband or wife constitutes grounds for divorce or abuse or murder. The choice to substitute "function" for "relationship and assessment of gifts" as the defining basis for distributing responsibility in a marriage or a family is surely the ultimate tragedy and plunges us back at least as far as the expulsion from Eden. I hope we do not need to start over again in the pits. See Hardenbrook, above, especially his discussion of the

"The Point of Great Debate," pp. 144-146, for a further discussion of "function" as distinct from "value" in demonstrating the need for men to control their wives. This modern heresy, linked perhaps to the Cartesian error by which fact and value were split, is fueled by the deep carnal need in both men and women to struggle for control of each other by using "power." Hardenbrook cites Elizabeth Gould Davis' nonsense about maleness being "a recessive genetic trait . . . abnormal . . . the Y chromosone is an accidental mutation boding no good for the race [an evidence of which is the fact] that killers and criminals are possessed of not one but *two* Y chromosones, bearing a double dose, as it were, of genetically undesirable maleness" (p. 106); but he fails to recognize that her reduction of maleness to a biological anomaly is a *functional* reductionism, not unlike his own appeal for male superior function in the family.

4. Daniel Levinson, et al., *The Seasons of a Man's Life* (New York: Ballantine, 1978).

5. Paul Wesley Chilcote, *Wesley Speaks on Christian Vocation* (Nashville: Discipleship Resources, 1986) pp. 2-3.

6. *Ibid.*, p. 3.

7. M. Scott Peck, *The Different Drum* (New York: Simon and Schuster, 1987) pp. 326-327.

8. James W. Fowler, *Becoming Adult, Becoming Christian: Adult Development and Christian Faith* (San Francisco: Harper and Row, Publishers, 1984) pp. 101-102.

9. *Ibid.*, pp. 103-105, from which I have summarized the characteristics of the mature Christian sense of vocation; I quoted him directly in the final item.

## Chapter Seven

1. See, for example, Robert L. Moore, *John Wesley and Authority*, V.H.H. Green, *The Young Mr. Wesley*, and James Fowler, "John

Wesley's Develoment in Faith," M. Douglas Meeks, editor, *The Future of the Methodist Theological Traditions* (Nashville: Abingdon, 1985) pp. 172-192.

2. What I have done here is to review my perceptions of David Ausubel's theory of adolescent development expressed in satellization terms. I have done so without referring again to the theory and the image which caught my attention in about 1968 when I was studying with Dr. Boyd McCandless at Indiana University. The book is a theoretical wonder of some 600 pages. The satellization material begins with chapter 7, "Personality Maturation During Adolescence," in his *Theory of Adolescent Development,* and continues throughout the remainder of the book at intervals where the model is needed to expand additional dimensions of Ausubel's theory of adolescent development.

## Chapter Eight

1. The C.S. Lewis anecdotal material is drawn entirely from *Surprised by Joy: The Shape of My Early Life* (London: Geoffrey Bles, 1955).
2. George Gallup, *Faith Development and Your Ministry* (Princeton: Religious Research Center, 1986).

## Chapter Ten

1. For fascinating information about brain organization and learning, see Leslie A. Hart, *How the Brain Works* (New York: Basic Books, 1975); see also his *Human Brain and Human Learning.* (New York: Longman, 1983).
2. Mildred Bangs Wynkoop, *A Theology of Love* (Kansas City: Beacon Hill, 1972).